# ONE STOP

# The One Stop Series

Series editor:  David Martin, FCIS, FIPD, FCB
                Buddenbrook Consultancy

A series of practical, user-friendly yet authoritative titles designed to provide a one stop guide to key topics in business administration.

Other books in the series to date include:

# ONE STOP
# *Marketing*

PATRICK FORSYTH

## ICSA Publishing
*The Official Publishing Company of*
*The Institute of Chartered Secretaries and Administrators*

in association with

## Prentice Hall Europe
London New York Toronto Sydney Tokyo Singapore
Madrid Mexico City Munich Paris

First published 1998 by
ICSA Publishing Limited
Campus 400, Maylands Avenue
Hemel Hempstead
Hertfordshire, HP2 7EZ

Typeset in 10/12.5 pt Meridien with Frutiger Light
by Hart McLeod, Cambridge

Printed and bound in Great Britain
by MPG Books Ltd, Bodmin, Cornwall

*British Library Cataloguing in Publication Data*

A catalogue record for this book is available from
the British Library

ISBN: 1-860-72060-9

1 2 3 4 5  02 01 00 99 98

They say that if you build a better mousetrap than your neighbour, people are going to come running. They are like hell! It's marketing that makes the difference.

Ed Johnson

# Contents

CONTENTS

For ease of reference, items which are definitions only (see p. xviii) are shown in italics above.

# *Preface*

*Because marketing is too important to
leave to marketing people . . .*

Despite its importance, marketing is widely misunderstood. When, over the years, I have regularly been asked what I do and have replied that I am in marketing, wrong assumptions have often been made. Other people do not have this problem. If someone says they are a dentist, say, people understand; they may not like the thought of it, but they understand. In a company too the function of many people is clear: the production manager keeps the production line moving, quality control speaks for itself, and the accountant keeps the score.

But marketing . . . it is, well, sort of advertising; or selling. Often people's first thoughts are followed by not only an inaccurate image but also a negative one – market traders, Brand X, supermarkets and too much 'junk' mail. Why is this? Marketing people believe marketing is important; if it is, then other people should know about it. Perhaps any confusion is the marketing peoples' fault. They should explain.

Does this matter? Yes, I believe it does, largely because so many people in an organisation are, wittingly or not, involved in, or affected by, marketing. Many have an influence on its effectiveness. And this is true from top to bottom of the organisation, in a whole range of departments and functions. So, it is important to any organisation that marketing is not isolated. It helps if it is widely understood; indeed, in competitive times, it must be understood if all are to play their part and marketing is going to be effective in 'bringing in the business'.

This book, one of a series arranged in an easy-to-access format, is designed to help make marketing clear to anyone in any position within any organisation. It is particularly directed at those in non-marketing functions and those new to, or considering entering, the marketing area. It sets out to demystify the term 'marketing' and the process it describes, to explain how the disparate elements of marketing work and how they interrelate to create a cohesive whole. It also aims to show why marketing is necessary, how it is important and what it can achieve.

Despite the overall A–Z format of the book, it is advisable to read the *Introduction* first as this provides a useful overview which will help keep matters in perspective when the reader is scanning any other section. Any specific links from one section to another are clearly shown.

Patrick Forsyth
Touchstone Training & Consultancy
28 Saltcote Maltings
Heybridge
Essex CM9 4QP

Spring 1998

# Introduction
## An overview of the nature and breadth of marketing and its role

Though marketing is to a degree a matter of common sense, it also involves complexity. For a start the word 'marketing' is used in (at least) five different ways. In addition, the various topics of this book – whose format dissects marketing and reviews aspects of it individually and, to some extent, in isolation – fit into the whole picture.

Without a clear overview, what is described in the following pages may sell the various individual aspects of marketing short. It is this overview, setting out the broad picture, that the introduction briefly describes. Its intention is to allow the reader subsequently to obtain more from their reading of the rest of the book.


## Scope and definition

Because of the confusion that sometimes surrounds marketing, we will start with a word about what marketing is not. It is not a euphemism for advertising, or a smart word for selling. Our first objective here is to demystify the word before looking at its relevance and application. Not only is marketing an area in which there is considerable jargon; it is also a word which is itself confusing because there are numerous definitions of it. The word is used in several different ways, and all are broader in scope and complexity than the euphemisms above.

In any business, marketing involves the following five elements: a concept, a function, a range of techniques, an ongoing process and a system.

1.  A *concept*: the belief that the customer is of prime importance in business, that success comes from customer orientation, seeing every aspect of the business through the eyes of the customer, anticipating their needs and supplying what they want in the way in which they want it; not simply trying to sell whatever we, as a company, happen to produce.

    This is surely no more than common sense (though manifestly not something every business embraces in its entirety) and is something that certainly always has relevance. In different businesses, of course, the 'customer' encompasses a number of different people. Goods or services may be sold direct to the public, or to them through others (wholesalers, retailers, etc.); other sorts of marketing involve other types of customer. For example, in business-to-business marketing, as the words suggest, one organisation sells to another.

2.  A *function* of business: to define it formally, 'the management function that is responsible for identifying, anticipating and satisfying customer requirements profitably'. In other words it is the process that implements the concept and, clearly, must be directed from a senior level and take a broad view of the business. More simply put, someone must wear the marketing 'hat'. In smaller companies, this may not be someone labelled 'marketing manager'; the responsibilities may lie with people such as a general manager, a sales manager, a promotion manager, or they may be – often are – shared amongst a number of people. Whoever is involved and however it is arranged, the final responsibility must be clear, and sufficient time must be found to fulfil all the necessary marketing functions.

3.  A *range of techniques*: not just selling and advertising but all those techniques concerned with implementing marketing in all its aspects. These include market research, product development, pricing and all the 'presentational' and promotional techniques such as selling, merchandising, direct mail, public relations, sales promotions, advertising, etc.

4.  An ongoing *process*: one that acts to 'bring in the business' by utilising and deploying the various techniques on a continuous basis; and doing so appropriately and creatively to make success more certain. Marketing is not a 'profit panacea'. It cannot guarantee success, nor can it be applied 'by rote' – the skill of those in marketing lies in precisely *how* they act in an area that is sometimes referred to, rightly, as being as much an art as a science.

So, what does marketing do to achieve its aims and lead an organisation through the potential minefield of external factors that may influence it? A little more about the continuous implementation of the marketing process will fit the range of techniques into the picture. This implementation must, if it is to be successful, be executed in a way that keeps a close eye on external factors. This cycle of activity is shown in Figure 1, and starts, unsurprisingly, with the customer. As the process goes on we can see how some of the classic marketing activities feature and how they relate to the concept in carrying out their specific rôle.

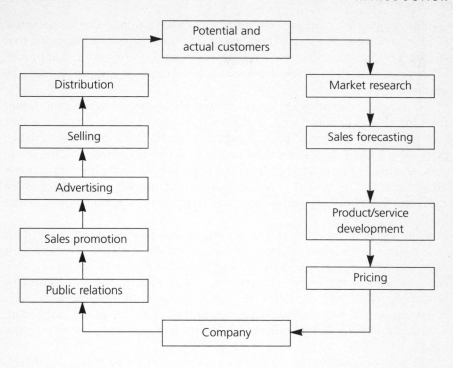

*Figure 1 The marketing process*

First, *market research* attempts to help identify, indeed anticipate consumer needs: what people want, how they want it supplied, and whether they will want it differently in the future. As research can analyse the past and review current attitudes, but not predict the future, it must concentrate on trends and needs careful interpretation. Even so it can have an important role in reducing risk and assisting innovation, and can be utilised throughout the marketing process not just as a preliminary.

Next, *sales forecasting* must be used to try to ascertain what quantity of a particular product/service may be purchased in future. Identifying a clear need is of little use commercially if only a handful of people want it. This is typical of areas where marketing does not offer exactitude. Forecasting is not easy – a point well made, albeit in another context, by the physicist Neils Bohr who said, 'Prediction is never easy; especially of the future' – and is never 100 per cent accurate; but the best estimate possible needs to be made to aid planning and reduce risk.

*Product and/or service development* is, for most businesses, a continuous process. Sometimes the process is more evolution than revolution, as a product gradually changes; sometimes it is more cosmetic than real (a new improved floor cleaner with ingredient X); sometimes it is so rapid that consumers get upset by the pace of obsolescence – as with computers, where it is said that, if you have the latest model, you know it must be obsolete.

No company can afford to stand still and innovation in marketing, rather than the slavish application of the status quo, must be the order of the day.

*Price*, and all aspects of pricing policy, is normally a marketing variable; price says a great deal about quality and must be set carefully. This is not only to ensure financial objectives are met, but to create the appropriate image and feeling of value for money in the market place. Price is an inherent part of the product/service and must be used as an element of the marketing process.

With these factors in place, the company must then *promote* itself externally; i.e. communicate, clearly and persuasively, to tell people what is available and encourage them to buy. A variety of techniques – *public relations, sales promotion, advertising,* etc. – can then be used, together or separately. Of all the promotional tactics, *selling* is the only personal one, involving one-to-one communication, and it often forms a final, important, link in the chain of different methods that connect the company to the market.

The impact of visibility is clear if you look at the history of many products as they have grown from small beginnings to be market leaders in their field; a process most often driven by the promotional investment made in them.

Lastly, a further important part of marketing, not yet mentioned, is *distribution*. Marketing sometimes involves a direct relationship: you see an advertisement in the newspaper and reply direct to the company, who send you the product; more often, there is a chain of intermediaries. Where did you obtain this book? Possibly direct from the publisher, but more likely from a bookshop, and possibly at a shop in a training, business or educational establishment of some sort. If so, the publisher may have sold it to a wholesaler (or distributor, library supplier, etc.) who in turn sold it to a bookshop. There are various possible chains that might operate here. Such situations are duplicated in many industries, so similarly, the new brake light bulb you buy for your car may go from the manufacturer to the wholesaler to the garage to you; other chains may be longer and there is often both complexity and change with which to contend.

5.  A *system*: one which involves variable factors that operate both inside and outside the marketing organisation. Many are restrictions. After all, an organisation cannot do just as it wants, ignoring the outside world; all sorts of factors may conspire to hinder its intentions. These factors

may range from competitive activity to government action.

The marketing system links the market (customers and potential customers) with the company, and attempts to reconcile the conflict between the two. A moment's thought will show that the objectives of company and customer are not the same. For example, the organisation may want to sell its products or services for a high profit, whereas the customer wants the best value for money.

Four elements comprise the marketing system and they position the marketing process within a broader context and link the organisation to the world outside. The four elements are:

- the company and its functions
- the market segments
- the marketing mix
- the external environment.

We will look here, briefly, at the company situation. The remaining three elements of the marketing system are examined in more detail in the main body of the text.

## The company and its functions

Every company has three basic functions – though in a well-directed company they do not operate in isolation from each other – and two major resources. The three basic functions are:

- production
- finance
- marketing.

The two major resources are:

- capital
- labour.

Each function has different tasks and different objectives, often operates on a different time-scale, attracts different types of people, and regards money in a different way. So, despite all contributing towards the same company objectives, there is inevitably internal conflict between, say, marketing and production (and thus the amount of product it is thought should be produced and what may be sold), or between production and finance.

> Note: Organisations, of course, vary. 'Production' usually implies factories and tangible products, but anything has to be produced. For example, software is not really in the same category as, say, a motor car but,

*equally, it has to be produced. Even the team of people who audit your company's accounts represent the production side of the accountancy firm who do the work. So both products and services are involved here.*

If you observe internal friction within your own company therefore, relax – you are normal. Figure 2 shows, in slightly caricatured form, how differences amongst people and functions affect the way things work.

|  | Finance | Production | Marketing |
|---|---|---|---|
| Objective | To ensure that the return on capital employed will provide security, growth and yield | To optimise cost/output relationships | To maximise profitable sales in the market place |
| Time period of operation | Largely past – analysing results plus some forecasting | Largely present – keeping production going particularly in 3-shift working | Largely future – because of lead time in reacting to market place |
| Orientation | Largely inward – concerned with internal results of company | Largely inward – concerned with factory facilities for personnel | Largely outward – concerned with customers, distribution and competition |
| Attitudes to money | Largely 'debit and credit' – once money spent, it is gone, money not spent is saved | Largely 'cost effective' – hence value analysis, value analysis techniques and cost cutting | Largely 'return on investment' – money 'invested' in promotion to provide 'return' in sales and profits |
| Personality | Often introverted: lengthy training; makes decisions on financially quantifiable grounds | Usually qualified in quantitive discipline; makes decisions on input/output basis | Often extroverted; often educationally unqualified; has to make some decisions totally qualitatively |

*Figure 2  How conflict arises between different organisational functions*

In many companies subcontraction is also involved and so the activity can spread outside the company itself. Marketing must, therefore, work within the constraints imposed by the way the company functions operationally or must to some extent. Profits are, after all, only generated *externally*; and the organisation as a whole must be structured in a way that allows marketing to be market-orientated. The market cares nothing for any internal inconvenience or confusion that may exist. It simply judges a company on its overall external image and the details that contribute to that. Thus things done for internal reasons that do not work in the market may dilute overall marketing effectiveness and so be damaging. Indeed, the 'sales' sometimes offer evidence of over-optimism on the part of marketing people.

The whole process or cycle of marketing is continuous, and we have already seen some of the different facets of marketing falling into place. Marketing, as we have already said, is as much an art as a science; it is a creative process which has some scientific basis, but no absolute guarantee of success. The customer is always fickle and unpredictable; marketing may be an exciting function of business, but it carries a real element of risk. On the other hand, when it goes well, it produces considerable satisfaction and it is at this stage, with a product selling well, that marketing people tend to become convinced that the success is *all* down to marketing. In fact, as this introduction shows, a wider range of influences is at work. It is because of this that it is often said that everyone in an organisation is involved in marketing; and there is a good deal of truth in this.

So, marketing is much more than simply a department, or a body of techniques; it is central to the whole reason for an organisation's being and to its relationship with its market and its customers. While, of course, many activities of a company are important, it is a truism to say that any kind of organisation can only create profits out in the market. So, unless marketing activity, in the fullest sense of the term, creates a situation where customers buy in sufficient quantity, producing the right revenue and doing so at the right time, no business operation will be commercially viable. Marketing has to produce a convincing reason for customers to buy, and make it a more powerful reason than that any competitor produces. Whatever the many elements involved, the key is to focus on customer needs and set out to satisfy them at a profit.

To summarise, and add a note of formality, let me record here that the Chartered Institute of Marketing has the following official definition of marketing: 'Marketing is the management process responsible for identifying, anticipating and satisfying customer requirement profitably'. Marketing guru Philip Kotler has defined it by saying: 'Marketing is the business function that identifies current unfulfilled needs and wants, defines and measures their magnitude, determines which target markets the organisation can best serve, and decides on appropriate products, services, and programmes to serve these markets. Thus marketing serves as the link between a society's needs and its pattern of industrial response'. These certainly express something of the complexity involved; marketing is more than just the 'marketing department'. Management guru Peter Drucker was content to say simply; 'Marketing is looking at the business through the customer's eyes', and indeed everything stems from exactly that.

So, already, with this introductory overview, it should be clear that there is more to marketing than may first meet the eye. This overview should help put the various elements in perspective, and the subsequent, A–Z, sections fill out the picture and add detail on individual elements. There are three types of entry in the book:

- main sections, each starting at the top of a page, identify major areas and comment on them in some depth
- boxed paragraphs, each headed Definition and arranged alphabetically, are intended to explain only briefly the term used in the heading
- definitions headings which simply direct the reader to details appearing in other related sections.

Together these give a clear picture of all the essentials of marketing. At the end of the book, the *Afterword* draws together the various entries covered.

---

### Key terminology

The text that follows is intended to span all forms of marketing. It is worth noting at the start the use of certain words and phrases:

*Consumer marketing:* This term is applied to the marketing of all products or services that are sold to ultimate customers, i.e. the things we all, as individuals, buy for ourselves, our home or family.

*Industrial marketing:* This implies marketing of products from industry to industry, e.g. the sale of machinery to a factory, or the sale of ball bearings for a machine sold on to a factory (the latter is sometimes called *component marketing*).

*Business-to-business marketing:* This is a broader term than industrial marketing, implying anything – product or service – that is sold by one business entity to another.

*Products:* These are what are sold; service companies will often refer to their 'products' and the word product is often used in the text to mean either product or service.

*Customer:* All organisations aim to sell their goods to customers, but customers are referred to differently in different businesses; service organisations more often talk about 'clients' (and other specific terms are also used, e.g. an airline refers to passengers).

Unless it is made clear to the contrary, most of the text is generally based and intended to apply to the broad span of marketing. So, unless an example is more specific, the points made will apply across the areas described above.

# *Added value*

**Introduction**

This is the concept of creating market advantage over competitors by enhancing the product and focusing attention on those elements of it that create special appeal to customers.

Added value can take the form of very practical factors, for example engineering features on a motor car that make it safer or less likely to break down. Or they can be, frankly, more cosmetic, for example the enhancing factors of a washing powder: *with added woomf 44*. Marketing must put over either or both, and sometimes seemingly minor cosmetic-sounding factors about a product *do* have importance for customers.

In some companies the main priority is the drive towards 'value added' and in industries which suffer from a pronounced case of the commodity factor (see *Introduction*) the constant need to keep even a marginal step ahead of competition in this way is very real.

# Advertising

## Introduction

Here we consider advertising, something we see all around us day by day. First a definition: advertising is 'any paid form of non-personal communication directed at target audiences through various media in order to present and promote products, services and ideas'. More simply, it can be called 'salesmanship in print or film'.

The role of advertising, as one of a number of variable elements in the communication mix, is 'to sell or assist the sale of the maximum amount of the product, for the minimum cost outlay'.

Advertising has various forms, depending on the role it is called upon to play among the other marketing techniques employed, in terms of both its type and the target to which it is directed. These include, by way of example:

- national advertising
- retail or local advertising
- direct mail advertising (and leaflets inserted in journals)
- advertising to obtain leads for sales staff
- trade advertising
- sector advertising (e.g. to a particular subdivision of a market such as the SoHo market – the Small office/Home office part of the market for computers and other office equipment).

A more specific way of understanding what advertising can do is by summarising some of the major purposes of advertising, i.e. the various and different objectives that can be achieved through using advertising in particular ways. These major purposes are to:

- inform potential customers of a new offering (from a new product to a product revision)
- increase the frequency of purchase
- increase the use of a product
- increase the quantity purchased
- increase the frequency of replacement

- lengthen any buying seasons
- present a promotional programme
- bring a family of products together
- turn a disadvantage into an advantage
- attract a new generation of customers
- support or influence a retailer, dealer, agent or intermediary
- reduce substitution by maintaining customer loyalty
- make known the organisation behind the range of offerings (corporate image advertising)
- stimulate enquiries (from customers or trade)
- give reasons why wholesalers and retailers should stock or promote a product
- provide 'technical' information about something (this may be actually technical or more general information).

There are clearly many reasons behind the advertising that you see around you. The purposes listed above are not mutually exclusive, of course, and many of those listed apply, or could apply, to one advertising campaign (though trying to do too much at once might risk diluting the effectiveness of any one element).

Whatever specific objectives the use of advertising seeks to achieve, its main tasks are usually to:

- gain the customer's attention
- attract customer interest
- create desire for what is offered
- prompt the customer to buy (either at once or in the future).

Advertising is, therefore, primarily concerned with attitudes and attitude change; creating favourable attitudes towards a product should be an important part of the advertising effort. Fundamentally, however, advertising also aims to sell, usually with the minimum of delay, although perhaps a longer time period may be needed in the case of informative or corporate (image-building) advertising.

Every advertisement should relate to the product or service, its market and potential market and, as a piece of communication, each advertisement can perform a variety of tasks. It may:

1. *Provide information*: This information can act as a reminder to current users or it can inform non-users of the product's existence.
2. *Attempt to persuade*: It can attempt to persuade current users to purchase again, non-users to buy for the first time and new users to change habits or suppliers.
3. *Create 'cognitive dissonance'*: Advertising can help to create uncertainty

about whether current suppliers can best satisfy needs. In this way, it can effectively persuade customers to try an alternative product or brand. (Extreme versions of this are referred to as 'knocking copy' – used sometimes by, among others, car manufacturers – and are openly critical of competition.)

4. *Create reinforcement*: Advertising can compete with competitors' advertising, which itself aims to create dissonance, to reinforce the idea that current purchases best satisfy the customer's needs. This maintains awareness and aims to continue to prompt ongoing purchases.

Moreover, advertising may also act to reduce the uncertainty felt by customers immediately after an important and costly purchase, when they are debating whether or not they have made the correct choice. This is perhaps most important with significant products and significant spending (e.g. a car or refrigerator) but is all part of constant reinforcement.

## Types of advertising

There are several basic types of advertising and these can be distinguished as follows:

1. *Primary*: This aims to stimulate basic demand for a particular product type – e.g. insurance, books, tea or wool – and includes advertising by overall trade bodies rather than individual suppliers.
2. *Selective*: This aims to promote an individual brand name, such as a brand of car, toilet soap or washing powder, which is promoted without particular reference to the manufacturer's identity.
3. *Product*: This aims to promote a product or range of related brands where some account must be taken of the image and interrelationship of all products in the mix.
4. *Institutional*: This covers public relations-type advertising which, in very general terms, aims to promote the company name, corporate image and the company services; it is broad advertising of an organisation, without mention of the various products or services that comprise its operation.

Advertising communicates through a variety of media, such as television and newspapers, and must be created and executed creatively with an appropriate strategy in mind if it is to be successful.

See also ADVERTISING MEDIA and ADVERTISING STRATEGY.

**Definition:** *Advertising agency*

Some firms do their own advertising, but more, especially the larger ones, tend to sub-contract the detailed and creative work entailed. An advertising agency is a specialist firm which creates advertising on behalf of its clients. The agency brings specialist skills of copy writing, design, media selection and buying, but must work closely with its clients; an understanding of the product and what advertising is trying to achieve is the key to making the relationship successful.

# *Advertising media*

**Introduction**

There is a bewildering array of advertising media available. Here we review some of the most popular methods of advertising, with a guide as to how they are used. All are potentially appropriate in any business, though the right mix for any one business will vary. For example, not every company can afford television advertising or wants the broad coverage it provides.

## Cosumer advertising

To paint a complete picture of the range of media available, the main categories which tend to provide good awareness amongst consumers are commented on in turn:

1. *Daily newspapers*: These, which often enjoy reader loyalty and, hence, high credibility, are particularly useful for prestige and reminder advertising. As they are read hurriedly by many people, lengthy copy may be wasted.
2. *Sunday newspapers*: These are read at a more leisurely pace and consequently greater detail can be included to good effect.
3. *Colour supplements* (and similar): Ideal for general advertising, but appeal to a relatively limited audience.
4. *Magazines*: These vary from quarterlies to weeklies and from very general, wide-coverage journals to many with a specific focus and some linked to very specialised interests. Similarly, different magazines of the same type (e.g. women's magazines) appeal to different age and socio-economic groups. Magazines are normally colourful and often read on a regular basis.
5. *Local newspapers*: Particularly useful (obviously) for anything local, but are relatively expensive if widely used for a national or broader campaign. They are sometimes used for test market area advertising support where a product is initially only made available on a limited basis.
6. *Television*: Regarded as the best overall medium for achieving mass impact and for creating an immediate or quick sales response. It is

arguable whether or not the audience is captive or receptive; but the fact that television is being used is often sufficient in itself to generate trade support. Television allows the product to be shown or demonstrated, is useful in test marketing new products because of its regional nature, but is very expensive – and therefore ruled out for most smaller companies.

7. *Outdoor advertising*: Lacks many of the attributes of press and television, but is useful for reminder copy and a support role in a campaign. Strategically placed posters near to busy thoroughfares or at commuter stations can offer very effective, long-life support advertising. Collaboration between suppliers and retailers can sometimes be used to link these to strategic locations designed to support local activity.

8. *Exhibitions*: Generate high impact at the time of the exhibition but, except for very specialised ones, their coverage of the potential market is low. They can, however, perform a useful long-term prestige role. In specific ways some can be very effective and in certain industries specific events are unmissable for serious players in the market.

> *Note: This is an area which overlaps with that of selling. Advertising needs to attract people to the exhibition, the design of the stand needs to create appropriate impact once inside, and the people 'on duty' need to play their parts well. For example, nothing deters visitors to an exhibition more quickly than the stereotyped 'Can I help you?' (to which the reply is usually: 'No thank you, I'm just looking'). Not only does personal input on the day have to be good; so too does the follow up. Exhibitions are hard work (as well as hard on the feet and the stomach!) but they can be very useful in generating business opportunities. For more detail, see* EXHIBITIONS.

9. *Cinema*: This, with its escapist atmosphere, can have an enormous impact on its audience of predominantly young people; but without repetition (i.e. people visiting the cinema once every week, or a tie-in with other media) it has little lasting effect. It is again useful for backing press and television, but for certain products only, bearing in mind the audience and the atmosphere. It is another medium where cost rules out the smaller company, though local advertising is possible by booking space in one individual cinema.

10. *Commercial radio*: This, playing music for every conceivable taste, or focusing on interest groups (e.g. news or phone-in enthusiasts) offers repetitive contact, has proved an excellent outlet for certain products, and is increasing the number of its users all the time. It is becoming

apparent that the new local radio stations appeal to a wide cross-section of people and thus offer support potential to a wide range of products. Many smaller companies are included among those who have tried this medium.

Not all these media (nor direct mail, reviewed later) are right for every product or in every circumstance. Some are simply not cost-effective in certain circumstances; you are unlikely to see, say, an individual small retailer advertising on television, but may well do so in a local newspaper or on a poster in the shopping precinct. Others assume greater importance because of their other linked characteristics: an advertisement alongside an editorial mention (perhaps generated by public relations activity – see PUBLIC RELATIONS) may work much better than one without this editorial link.

Every advertiser must make individual decisions (advertising agencies who handle the larger advertising budgets have sophisticated media-buying departments), not only about different methods, but about exact media – one particular newspaper rather than another, and so on.

Not all advertising, however, is aimed at potential consumers; some is directed at intermediaries, as outlined below.

## Trade advertising

This is certainly important, and in many industries advertising is split between that directed to ultimate customers and that directed at those in the channels of distribution involved in their being able to purchase. It is often not sufficient to advertise products to consumers alone, particularly where it is important that distributors/retailers are willing to stock and promote a product.

Even though the sales force has a prime role to play in ensuring that stocking and promotion objectives are achieved, trade advertising also has an important role to play in this respect; indeed it sets the scene for such sales visits. Trade advertising can:

- remind retailers/distributors about the product between sales visits
- keep them fully informed and up-to-date on developments and changes of policy
- alleviate problems associated with the cold-call selling of less well-known products
- indicate the support and weight being given to a product; this is disproportionately important within many trades, being used both as an objective measure of assessing what stocking to decide upon, and as

an easy – albeit subjective – measure to making a quick decision to
stock.

Often trade advertising occurs prior to, or linked to, consumer advertising
campaigns to help prompt the buying-in of stock in anticipation of future
demands to be created by the consumer advertising. Other tactics link in.
For example, when new products are launched or special promotions
introduced, trade support may be achieved through special offers (e.g. if
you order a minimum of 24, promotional support of some sort is included)
or increased (introductory) discounts, all of which can be effectively
emphasised by trade advertising.

This type of advertising can also communicate to the trade the detail of
the moment – why they should stock forthcoming lines or reorder existing
ones – as well as flag the timing and weight of any advertising or other
support (press coverage, feature on radio, etc.) that is to come.

Curiously, perhaps one of the most important aspects of trade advertising
is not what it says (though I do not intend to suggest it does not matter
what is said or how it is put over – it does) but *the fact that it is there*. The
commitment (and cost) of taking such space is seen by many as a
commitment to particular products or promotions. If a sales representative
is pressing a buyer to take large stocks, mount a window display or
generally take a product seriously, then the buyer is apt to ask, quite
reasonably, 'What are you doing for it?' This is a genuinely important aspect
of trade advertising.

Even so, the advertising mix deployed here, whether it is directed to
products, to the company, to a range or to any combination of these, must
accommodate this fact. The more retailers feel that a supplier is matching
their views of potential success with action, the more they are likely to
respond positively to stocking suggestions.

Advertising effort needs to be spread amongst the various target
audiences that match a particular product. Trade advertising may take a
large share of this on occasion. It must be tailored to the trade, who
probably want to hear different things from the ultimate public and
potential customers, and be spoken to in a different way. The basic
principles of what makes advertising work and the strategy involved are
similar for all types of advertising. See ADVERTISING for an overview, and
ADVERTISING STRATEGY for more detail of how advertising media are
used.

# *Advertising strategy*

See also ADVERTISING (for an introduction and overview) and ADVERTISING MEDIA.

> **Introduction**
>
> Advertising is more than a series of individual advertisements. It reflects, or should do, an overall gameplan – a strategy, which coordinates what is done, producing a cohesive whole directed at achieving the desired results.

Advertising needs to be designed and produced in a way that reflects an analysis of the market and a subsequent sensible choice of media and of advertising strategies. This means that those involved – often more than one person – must be in close communication.

If advertising effectiveness is to be maximised then it must be carefully planned and originated. It may help to spell out what needs to be done in a simple strategy document. At its best, such an advertisement strategy statement is brief and economical, and does its job in three paragraphs describing:

- the basic proposition – the promise to the customer and the statement of benefit
- the 'reason why' or support proof justifying the proposition, the main purpose of which is to render the message as convincing as possible
- the 'tone of voice' in which the message should be delivered – the image to be projected and, not infrequently, the picture the customer has of himself/herself, which it could be unwise to disturb or, rather, wise to capitalise on.

In various fields some of the finest and most effective advertising has sometimes been produced without reference to any advertising strategy, or for that matter without knowledge of real market facts. However, although research or objective thinking cannot always give all the details, or for that matter always be infallibly interpreted, it can give strong indications and reduce the chances of failure.

Most executives, when faced with a rough or initial visual and copy layout, have an automatic subjective response: 'I like it/I don't like it'. And while the creator may attempt to explain that the appraiser is not a member of the target audience, it can be genuinely difficult to be objective. Nevertheless, while an attempt at objectivity must be made, there are few experienced advertising or marketing executives who can say that their judgement has never let them down. Advertising remains as much an art as a science. (The most famous saying about advertising is that of the company chairman who remarked, 'I know half the money I spend on advertising is wasted, but I do not know which half' – which contains a good deal of truth, and is a sobering thought in the context of many organisations where every penny of a budget has to be fought for.)

Another possible problem in any business is that of what is called 'me-tooism'. Advertising gets into a rut; those producing it simply reiterate an established formula and stop even trying to think creatively. This gives rise to 'tombstone-style' advertisements saying little and saying it uncreatively. Easy to produce, low cost, yes – but hardly likely to have major or striking impact. Such might be judged fine as an announcement to the faithful (those who will buy the product almost automatically), but surely much advertising is, or should be, designed to do more than that. It is one thing for it to be there and visible; it is quite another for it to be *persuasive*.

---

**Warning**

There is also a danger of confusing creativity, the process that makes something both appropriate to customers and memorable, with cleverness. Sometimes a clever idea – a play on words in a headline, perhaps – can act not to increase the power of the advertisement, but to dilute it or obscure what should be a clear message. Advertising must never fall into the trap of confusing cleverness with clarity of communication.

---

All companies should ask straight questions about their advertising style generally and also in particular. Such questions include:

- Does the advertisement match the strategy laid down?
- Does the advertisement gain attention and create awareness?
- Is it likely to create interest and understanding of the advantages of the product it offers?
- Does it create a desire for the benefits of the product and really prompt the need to buy?
- Is it likely to prompt potential clients to make a purchase, either now or in the future?

- Can it be linked to tangible action, e.g. does it have a coupon to complete and return or a 'hotline' telephone?
- Does it concentrate on the features of the product, rather than benefits to the reader/purchaser?

In other words: does the advertising communicate? Will people notice it, understand it, believe it, remember it and buy as a result of it?

The next question is how can an advertisement be made creative? There are many ways: using humour, personalities, exotic locations, cartoons, even running advertisements in serial form, ending with a cliff-hanger to encourage viewing the next episode. (Gold Blend coffee was the first to use this form, on television, and even ran press advertisements giving no more than the time and date of the next instalment; the campaign was very successful and shows that new ideas can be found, and that sales can rise as a result.)

So, advertising needs to be creative. Often its task is to make something which is routine, or even potentially dull, 'interestingly different'. Just occasionally the product really is interestingly different; more often, the essential qualities of the product need presenting in a persuasive way.

## Advertising approaches

The following, invented, example * reviews the options in a way that makes clear the approaches involved, albeit in a light-hearted way.

Sometimes the product is such that, with no competition and with a perfect match to customers' needs, all the advertisement has to do is say what the product will do for them: *'New instant petrol – one spoonful of our additive to one gallon of water produces petrol at 1p a gallon'*. If your message is like this, there is no problem – persuasion is inherent in the message. But few products are like this. It is more likely that any product will have competition of one sort or another. Then you have to say more about it; or start by thinking of everything about it. You may even say everything about it:

> SPLODGE – *the big, wholesome, tasty, non-fattening, instant, easily-prepared, chocolate pudding for the whole family.*

Or you may stress one factor, thereby implying that your competitors' products are lacking in this respect:

* adapted from *Everything You Need To Know About Marketing*, by Patrick Forsyth, Kogan Page, 1995.

*SPLODGE – the easily-prepared pudding.*

Customers may know all puddings of this sort are easy to prepare, but they are still likely to conclude yours are easiest. The trouble with this approach is that in a crowded market there are probably other puddings already being advertised as 'easily prepared'. And 'big', 'wholesome' and all the rest for that matter. What then? Well, one way out is to pick a non-essential factor which may have been ignored by your competitors:

*SPLODGE – the pudding in the ring pull pack.*

It may be a marginal factor but your advertisement now implies it is important and that competition is lacking. Alternatively, you can pick a characteristic of total irrelevance:

*SPLODGE – the pudding that floats in water.*

Or link it to the pictorial side of the advertisement:

*SPLODGE – the pudding you can eat on top of a bus.*

If competition has done all of this then you have only one alternative: you must feature in the advertisement something else, which has nothing to do with the product. This may even necessitate giving something away:

*SPLODGE – the only pudding sold with a **free** sink plunger.*

Or re-packaging:

*SPLODGE – the only pudding in the **transparent** ring pull pack.*

The possibilities are endless and the ultimate goal is always to make your product appear different, attractive and, thereby, desirable.

In addition to all this, advertising has to be made to *look* attractive. Sometimes this may be achieved through added humour, use of personalities, etc. Equally, it can be achieved through lavish production expenditure – commissioning special photography may be costly, but the quality may immediately create something special. A danger here is that the 'pluses' hide the message: viewers of a poster, say, may laugh at its humour but may not recall exactly what it was advertising.

Not surprisingly, standards vary. Some advertising does tend to be routine, with much of it taking the form of little more than an announcement of a product's existence. In increasingly competitive times more creative approaches may need to be explored and may pay dividends.

This is an area where new ideas are always, indeed must be, in evidence and where much of the marketing battle can be won or lost.

# *Branding*

## Introduction

A product needs a name. Simplistically, this can be something like 'Bloggs Biscuits', and require no more thinking than remembering your own name. More often in marketing the intention is to create a product characterised and made memorable by its name, so that the combination of name, product and product characteristics – including subjective factors such as image – is part of what motivates people to buy.

Sometimes this is achieved with a simple name; Smiths Crisps continue to do well despite a very simple approach to their name. Sometimes agencies are employed, midnight oil is burnt and a name is only decided upon after long deliberation. There are all sorts of considerations: is it catchy, easy to pronounce, does it look good in print, does it work internationally (and not have some unfortunate meaning, see OVERSEAS MARKETING)? But there are no rules. Who would have thought a name like 'I Can't Believe It's Not Butter' (for a butter-like spread) would work? It is surely far too long, but it does work, at least for the moment, and has inspired other extra-long names.

Companies work at this process and names may change and evolve over time. BMW certainly sounds better than Bavarian Motor Company, and such reduction is not uncommon; British Telecom has also reduced its name to BT, for example. There are many different approaches to name, and there is more to a brand than just a name.

Branding encapsulates the whole concept of creating a product and giving it an appealing image (one often targeted at a specific group of customers, see MARKET SEGMENTS). It gives rise to various jargon phrases used to define the subsidiary processes involved:

1.  *Brand image*: The image that goes with the total product/brand creation, e.g. the identification of Audi cars with excellence of engineering and thereby with performance, safety, and so on; it is the detail of this definition and analysis that links to the implementation of exactly how the marketing of the brand takes place and evolves over time.

2. *Brand positioning*: This refers to the position of a particular brand on a 'scale' of similar, competing, brands and determines how high/low a price should be set, how popular/exclusive it should be, how practical/fashionable, etc.

3. *Brand personality*: This is a slant on brand image and emphasises the character of the product rather than its more tangible aspects.

4. *Brand extension*: A term referring to a particular use of branding. Brands tend to be equated with particular products and, if successful, they create a powerful force for sales, building loyalty and making repeat sales more successful. Brand extension takes a franchise in the market and uses it to create products in different areas; these products gain from the image created for the original brand name. The following examples make the concept clear:

   • Mars bars – Mars ice cream (different, but not so different a product area)
   • Porsche cars – Porsche watches (very different)
   • Virgin airline – cola and bridal shops (again very different).

   You can probably think of other examples. There is a strategic choice here. Not all companies operate this way, and too much brand extension can become confusing for the customer and thus self-defeating.

4. *Brand values*: This refers to the need to keep a brand's personality within bounds and not to over-extend the image by trying to make it all things to all people; it would, for example, be over-extending brand values for Rolls Royce to promote their high-quality cars as the best vehicle in which to nip to the shops.

Branding tends to be applied most often to FMCG (Fast Moving Consumer Goods) products, but the concept applies equally in other areas and is relevant and referred to in industrial and business-to-business products, e.g. computers (which perhaps combine aspects of both consumer and industrial products) and even jet engines for an airline.

# *Buyers*

**Introduction**

All marketing is directed towards buyers. What exactly that word implies can vary, but the precise nature of the buyers in any particular industry is important and marketing must focus on it.

The following brief comment tries to clarify the range of people included under the heading 'buyer'. Various terms are used: general ones, such as customers and clients (particularly for services) and more specific ones, such as guests for a hotel and passengers for an airline. All these people buy, but 'buyers' is a word that often implies a 'professional' buyer – more usual in industrial marketing. The person who buys soap for a supermarket group is a buyer; the shopper who buys it in the shop is a customer. Customers in this sense may sometimes be called consumers.

A potential customer is called a 'prospect', especially if the contact with them is a sales one (sales people visit prospects).

The terminology is not precise here but the main difference to bear in mind is between customers in the 'Joe Public' sense, and professional buyers who are fewer in number, but equally fickle and demanding.

**Definition:** *Channels of distribution*

See DISTRIBUTION.

**Definition:** *Competition*

Competition is just one of many restrictions on marketing activity. Clearly marketing cannot go about its business as if the rest of the world does not exist. See EXTERNAL FACTORS.

# Consumerism

**Introduction**

This term is perhaps the flip side of marketing. Marketing must always focus more on the customer and their needs than on how the customer views the way of doing business; it must take care not to make the customer feel pressurised or disadvantaged in any way.

Like so much else associated with marketing, 'consumerism' originated in the United States with the work of consumer champion Ralph Nader. Gradually consumers were encouraged to become more critical, more demanding and to consider their rights; this was in contrast to the old way of *caveat emptor* – let the buyer beware.

Two specific consequences of all this are worth noting. First, the safety aspect (Ralph Nader came to fame largely because of his work on raising car safety standards) which must essentially be good. No one wants a medicine, say, to be marketed before it is well tested. And marketing of many products is now affected by controls, legislation and other forms of agreement to ensure standards are met. Sometimes this produces a bonus for marketing. For example, an amendment strengthening the law on the safe wear level of car tyres immediately produces extra business.

A second consequence is more opportunistic. Many organisations play to the prevailing culture of consumerism, using it to strengthen their image and thus their sales. A simple early example of this is the Marks & Spencer policy of allowing easy return and exchange of goods, which must clearly increase the volume of business in present buying – and that is just one effect. Other examples range from special guarantees, safety inspections and product innovations linked to safety (e.g. ABS brakes on cars).

**Warning**

Consumerism is an area that needs care; the danger of running foul of consumers is expensive and, at worst, can damage reputations beyond repair.

# Customer care

**Introduction**

Customer service, as customers both anticipate and experience it, is fundamental to sales and marketing success. It is no overstatement to suggest that customer care is the foundation that underpins ongoing marketing success. The whole process involved is nowadays more often called customer care.

## The necessity for excellence in customer care

As has already been mentioned (in the Introduction and elsewhere), it is increasingly difficult for customers to differentiate between many competing products in the market. In many industries, products are essentially similar in terms of design, performance and specification, at least within a given price bracket. This is as true of industrial products as of consumer goods. Often, therefore, customers' final choices will be influenced by more subjective factors. Customer service can play a major role in final choice, sometimes becoming the most important factor.

For example, in the author's own business, the source of ring binders used for the many courses and seminars we run was, for a while, influenced almost exclusively (in a commodity-type product area with many suppliers offering similar products) by the efficiency and customer orientation of one person in the supplier's sales office. When this person left the company, our business was moved elsewhere. The antithesis of this is the 'abominable noman' who too often seems to inhabit the sales office and can destroy months of work by management and sales staff, miss opportunities and lose orders, or indeed customers, in one brief telephone call. Everyone has a favourite horror story, a fact which may say something about prevailing standards.

**Warning**

Any shortfall in prevailing standards presents an opportunity for others in an industry to take advantage and steal the edge in the market.

It is not a question of aiming for some idea of perfection (after all both McDonald's restaurants and the Ritz Hotel would claim to offer good service, but in very different ways – and they are both right to say so) but any company must organise things positively to achieve the standards they have decided that they – or rather their customers – require.

So, what creates good customer care? It comes primarily through the careful consideration of both staffing and organisation. It is not easy. The mix of characteristics and considerations that can help make success more likely is not easy to define. It is not enough:

- for the manager responsible for support areas only to be a good administrator, although without the sorting out of priorities, without smooth handling of enquiries, files, paperwork, correspondence and records, sales support will never be effective
- for the manager only to be a good sales person, although it is essential to have an understanding or familiarity with sales techniques, to be able to recognise sales opportunities, and to ensure that they and all members of their team meet them
- only to be an effective manager of people, although it is vital to be able to lead and motivate a close-knit and enthusiastic team, tackling a diverse range of activities in hectic conditions.

The manager also has to understand and pass on an understanding of the role of sales support, so that all concerned see it as a vital tactical weapon in the overall marketing operation. This means that they must have an appreciation of what marketing is and the various ways in which, directly or indirectly, the sales office, and sales support or customer care staff can contribute to company profitability.

This implies a knowledge of, and involvement in, the marketing process. For example, if sales support personnel are not told (or do not ask) about the relative profitability of different products, they may be busy pushing product A when product B, similar in price or even more expensive, makes more money.

A pre-requisite for contributing effectively is for any manager to be able to identify priorities. With such a variety of activities, with incoming calls and enquiries being so unpredictable, the manager either adheres to rigid sets of rules that allow things to be coped with and runs an adequate office, or he or she has the skill and initiative to recognise different priorities and to get the best out of them, so building up a really effective operation.

Identifying priorities is of little use, however, unless the manager is able to deal with them in an organised way. This calls for ability in managing and controlling time, systems and people. To be effective, the manager must be a consistent sales-orientated manager of people, able to accept ideas from others, able to cope with the problems of the urgent and balance them against the opportunities of the important. There is an important link here with the various electronic systems used in customer service. It is not untypical these days for a company to be able to call up a customer's full details on screen instantly by tapping in just their account number or post code. So systems must be organised in every possible way to facilitate customer service, and yet how often do complaining customers hear systems – and policy – blamed for a company's inability to give proper customer service?

The sales support team must be organised to produce an ongoing positive cycle of repeat business from its contacts. Even negative contacts such as complaints can be dealt with as part of a positive cycle involving a range of possible contacts with the customer, either directly or through other sections of the company. Although possibly low among company priorities, sales support in fact occupies a central position and is vital in terms of contacts and influence.

For this to occur may require close and constructive co-operation with other sections of the company, for example, with production, or with the sales force. Poor liaison can cause problems. In one company, for instance, sales office staff spent time handling complaints about delivery on 75 per cent of orders that went through, not because delivery was bad, but because the sales force was quoting six weeks delivery when everyone in the company knew it was normally eight weeks. Such unnecessarily wasted time could be used more constructively to increase sales.

There are, of course, exceptions, but prevailing standards of sales office service and selling are often not high – or not as high as they could be. It should not be difficult to make customer contact stand out in a way that not only impresses customers but which also genuinely increases sales results. For many firms, this is a real opportunity area that is too often neglected.

There are no excuses for not selling. Time pressure, work pressure, staffing, equipment and resources may all make it more difficult, but what ensures that real selling does take place is, first, attitude and, second, skills and knowledge of how to do it effectively. Only management can get this over and maintain standards. It is, in fact, much easier to run a 'tight ship', to set standards and stick to them, than to let things go by default. People are motivated by belonging to the 'best team' and come to care very much about standards and performance.

Selling must not be confused with simple customer service, however efficient and courteous. This is not to deny the vital importance of service and courteousness. These form one of the bases for success, but so does product knowledge – not just knowing about the product, but being able to

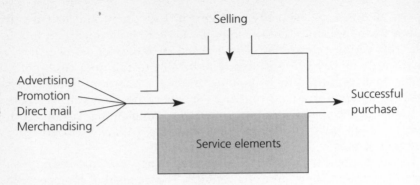

*Figure 3  Sales are the net result of promotion, selling and good service*

talk about it in such a way that makes sense to the customer. This does not just happen. Management must ensure that it does, and similarly with sales technique. The sales office team (all of them who have customer contact) must have a basic knowledge of the sales process augmented by a knowledge of and ability to apply particular skills, on the telephone or in letter writing for instance, and backed as necessary by sheer persistence and inventiveness.

Again, this does not just happen. Management is responsible for recruiting the right people, for their initial training and on-going development, and for motivating them on a continuous basis. As with so many topics reviewed here, customer service and the internal sales effort have more to them than meets the eye. Yet think about organisations you do business with, as a company or as an individual. There is always one about which you say 'never again!', and others where good service draws you back time after time, probably without your thinking that you have been sold to in a 'pushy' manner.

Promotion, selling and customer care act together to produce the right level of business; this is illustrated in Figure 3, where the various influences are like water flowing into a tank, with the outflow (sales) the net result of them all.

## Influence of backup activities on sales

Sales people may succeed or fail largely through their own personal approaches, but they are necessarily dependent on the quality of the product or service which they sell, and the image of the company for which they sell it. So, if your job is involved with anything to do with either, then you help influence sales success.

This is more than saying that those on the production line are involved, there are many more specific circumstances. Consider a few examples of how people in an organisation, who might feel they have little or no relationship with 'marketing', can influence things:

- someone in technical support, handling a customer query, will not only sort out the problem, but influence the likelihood of a customer re-ordering
- someone responsible for originating a computer system which, ultimately, interfaces with customers will affect company image and thus the sales person's relationship with customers
- someone in accounts, sorting out VAT on a customer account, affects the image of the company for good or ill.

In some of these areas a customer's expectation, often based on experience, is that any good impression of the company will be dispelled. Who, hearing the words 'it's in the computer', does not expect some inconvenience? What equivalents of this do you have in your own organisation?

The marketing orientated organisation loses no opportunity to maximise both customer care and sales.

# Database marketing

## Introduction

This is jargon for a particular variety of marketing; an approach which is based on all the other principles of marketing, yet has a special focus of its own.

Database marketing is simply marketing that is actioned off a database of customer names. It implies a reasonably personal style of communication (see also RELATIONSHIP MARKETING) and covers a range of situations: a department store's regular communications with account holders is database marketing (probably to customers only) and so may be what a bank does primarily by direct mail communication with customers and prospects (see DIRECT MAIL).

The intention here is to develop the customer base over time, creating greater loyalty, selling the range and maintaining the relationship as the nature of the organisation and what it provides changes (in part to keep pace with customer expectations).

## Warning

The more personally marketing is directed, the more harshly it will be judged if it is inaccurate. Matching records and message is vital; if a customer is contacted in a way that ignores or makes mistakes with regard to previous communication then it will strike them (rightly) as inefficient and the impact will be diminished accordingly.

# *Design*

**Introduction**

Design is an inherent part of any product (and the same can be said of services in a less tangible way). It is not just about making something practical or 'nice'; it is a marketing variable and can be used to enhance marketing effectiveness.

Design links closely to product quality. It is a variable and so can be used in a marketing context to differentiate. Design may link to fashion, it may simply be very distinctive, or it may combine both qualities as in, say, Swatch watches. Design may have its own appeal, albeit a subjective one, meaning that design desirability is an additional reason to buy something; or it may – indeed often does – have practical connotations. Looking good and performing well are important considerations in a wide range of products – from fax machines to electric razors. Where design is important, marketing and technical and design departments need to work well – and closely – together.

**Warning**

If design forges ahead without allowing for marketing considerations then the end result may be like Sir Clive Sinclair's C5, an electric 'car' quickly dubbed the electric bedroom slipper, and be even more quickly removed from the market. Of course, there are dangers the other way round; marketing alone will never be able to make a badly designed product a commercial success. And products can be over-designed, thereby pricing themselves out of the market.

As with so much else in marketing, balance is vital, and achieving it can be difficult – hence the earlier description of marketing as both art and science.

## Introduction

Direct mail is a very particular form of advertising. Although it is, in effect, just a different form of advertising (and some of what is said under that heading applies here) it is sufficiently important to merit its own entry. It is an important, useful, flexible and effective medium.

Direct mail has a mixed reputation, yet only the worst of it should be called 'junk mail'*. Some perhaps deserves that description; as Samuel Johnson said, 'What is written without effort, is in general read without pleasure'. It can be directed at any level of the buying process, from ultimate customers to specialist retailers (it is sometimes useful for customers who do not justify the cost of personal sales visits, or more than a certain number of visits). It is also relevant throughout industrial and business-to-business marketing, and people may receive as many mail shots on their desks at work as they do on their doormat at home.

Despite its prevalence and usefulness, feelings about direct mail sometimes run high. Some people regard it as intrusive. Everyone seems to know someone who has been mailed three times in the same week about something entirely inappropriate, and addressed wrongly as 'Dear Madam'. Other people regard it as more than intrusive, ranking somewhere between picking your teeth in public or being unkind to animals.

Direct mail is, though, only a form of advertising – no more, no less, albeit a specialised form. It is used very successfully in a wide range of industries and applications, many of them perfectly respectable, such as charities, banks and building societies. Many others are dependent on it as their main form of promotion or because it results in a major proportion of their sales (indeed, one example is sales of business books such as this). What is more, although there is the occasional exception, direct mail is

---

* One class of decidedly junk mail is the increasing number of communications that now arrive by fax. When sent cold, these are totally self-defeating; they tie up the customer's line, use their paper and cost them money. Most people resent such communications deeply and their use is not recommended.

31

used, for the most part, without upsetting the people to whom it is directed. Indeed, some will even pay to receive it. The author pays to receive mailings from the Barbican and for various catalogues, such as *The Good Book Guide*. If people are not interested, they throw direct mail material away – a process which is not unlike turning over a magazine page containing an advertisement in which one is not interested. Of course direct mail is wasteful and it hurts to think of so many carefully penned words ending up in the bin. But it is no more wasteful than other forms of advertising. All advertising is in a sense wasteful – what matters is whether it produces a cost-effective response, whether it pays for itself in the long term.

Contrary to popular belief, direct mail is nearly always opened and much of it is read. In the UK, the Post Office, which spends a great deal of time and money studying the effectiveness of direct mail, recently demonstrated through research that more than 90 per cent of it is opened and more than 75 per cent of it is read. The trick for users of direct mail, therefore, is to ensure that their offering will stand out from others, will generate interest and will be seen as persuasive.

Direct mail is not an alternative to advertising; rather it adds to the range of techniques available. It is no more a magic formula than any other individual technique. But it can sometimes suit well. It is flexible; certainly more flexible than advertising. Direct mail may mean either four letters, or 40, 400, 4,000 or 40,000. It does not have to be done on the grand scale, it can be targeted at small specific groups; it can be undertaken progressively with so many shots per week or month being sent, which is useful for small companies. It is personal and can be directed at specific and discrete groups – not just farmers, but arable farmers with more than 1,000 acres in East Anglia, for instance. It is controllable, it can be tested, implemented progressively and results can be monitored to ensure it provides a cost-effective element in the total promotional mix. As it is likely to be low-cost per contact, and because campaigns can be varied so much in size, there are few organisations which could not experiment with the technique. It can be specific or it may be directed broadly, selling the firm, or being part of the promotion of particular products or services.

It can aim to do various things, for example:

- prompt an order (fill in the form, send a cheque and the goods follow)
- prompt requests for more information: brochures, etc.
- arrange an appointment for a sales person to visit
- encourage customers to visit everything from shops to exhibitions where purchase can be completed
- link to demonstrations, samples, showroom visits, etc.; it is as important in multi-stage selling, to move the process on to another stage, as it is in situations where stimulating an order is the immediate intention.

So, direct mail has many advantages. It is a proven technique in many fields. It can be used on a small scale, it can be targeted on specific market segments, and it can be tested and monitored much more easily than many other forms of promotion. But it is also deceptive and can appear easier to use than, in fact, it is. Every element of it needs careful consideration.

Among the components of direct mail are:

1. *The list*: Any mailing is only as good as the list of names it is mailed to. It must be appropriate, up-to-date and personal. Mailings addressed to an individual do best. In many businesses existing customers are as important as prospects, so complex overlapping campaigns are constructed; there is a specialised area of 'database marketing' and, though list-holding and use is now covered by the Data Protection Act in the UK, sources of lists are valuable. Next time you are asked in a store to write your name and address on the back of the cheque, list-building may be the reason. Other techniques, such as satisfaction cards, are specifically designed as list-builders.

2. *The message*: This is vital. Copywriting in this area is a specialist job. Just one phrase changed can increase (or decrease) the response. There are about three seconds, when something is pulled out of an envelope, during which the recipient decides whether or not to read on, so immediate impact is crucial.

3. *The envelope*: This is part of the message. Many envelopes are overprinted, perhaps with a 'teaser' message, often a question; what is on them affects response and is particularly important in getting the recipient to read on, and to do so in the right frame of mind.

4. *The letter*: This is vital and is often not short. A good message is as long as is necessary to present an argument to buy, and if this takes two or three pages so be it; many long letters work well. As a general rule, a brochure and a letter together produce a better result than a brochure on its own.

5. *Brochures*: These provide supporting information in a variety of ways. They may be coloured, illustrated and, in extreme cases, incorporate a range of gimmicks from prize draws to stamps.

Direct mail is a technique where tiny details matter. For instance, a letter with a PS at the end may do better than one without; a reply card with an actual postage stamp (rather than with prepaid postage) may get up to 50 per cent more replies; and certain 'magic' words (new, free, guaranteed, exciting) seem to boost response, provided they are not overused.

> *Note:* *The copy – all the text, that is, whether in a letter or a brochure – may not necessarily be read in order or at one sitting. People dip in and out of material, so some repetition of content between, say, letters and*

*brochures (though perhaps not actual words) may be sensible. Certainly the relationship between what is said in different elements of the mailing needs careful consideration.*

## An example

Because of the importance of direct-mail technique it is worth taking time to exemplify how it works. *The Good Book Guide* would not exist unless it made direct mail work; direct mail is its main form of promotion. One of their letters is reproduced below (see Figure 4). It is a good example of an approach that works well; it is clear, punchy and makes you want to read on. The letter makes a clear offer and gives an incentive to action. It is in full colour and is accompanied by a reply-paid envelope and a high-quality reply form which repeats some of the message. The whole shot is well-conceived and well-produced.

The author is grateful to Jeremy Brown, marketing director of The Good Book Guide, for permission to use the letter and also for his comments on the promotion. He explains as follows:

The Good Book Guide has always been an intriguing marketing challenge. A product for a global market – people who want to read good books published in the UK – we are neither a book club nor a book distributor. Our core activity is the process of selection and recommendation. We sift through all the books published in the UK, subject the good and promising ones to the scrutiny of our panel of independent reviewers and publish only the best of the resultant reviews. Our foundation source of revenue has been, from day one, the sale of a subscription magazine (now monthly) containing selections of the best titles. I use the word 'foundation' deliberately, because the majority of our income comes from the sale of the products themselves to our subscribers (we buy in and stock copies of every title for which we publish a review). But we don't get access to that sales income unless we have a subscriber base.

So, there's the challenge; to walk the tightrope between the *quality*-driven process of review and selection on the one hand and the *quantity*-driven process of product sales on the other.

Current approaches reflect a number of recent changes. When the guide started out, nearly 20 years ago, our readers were almost exclusively English ex-pats. Today, as a substantial (and continually growing) proportion of our customer base is made up of people for whom English is a second language, the dominance of the old 'ex-British colony' geographic bias is waning. Customer distribution is becoming

*'The great thing about The Guide remains its complete impartiality and lack of gimmicks and pressure on the one hand, together with its firm commitment to books, authors... and the all-important customers on the other.'*

**THE DAILY TELEGRAPH**

*Dear Reader*

If you love books, as I do, you'll know how hard it is to keep up to date with the flood of new titles that appear each month. Which ones are worth reading? And how can you buy them easily?

As Editor of The Good Book Guide, I'd like to introduce you to a wonderful solution to both these problems - our worldwide book review and delivery service.

### Special introductory offer

The enclosed leaflets describe the service and how it works. If you like what you see simply fill in and return the enclosed subscription order form to receive:

- 12 issues of The Good Book Guide Magazine, our monthly review of the best new books
- 12 issues of the GBG Extra, the feature supplement published with each issue of the Magazine
- Subscriber only Special Offers every month
- Free copies of the next two issues of The Good Book Guide Catalogue - a comprehensive round-up of the best titles in print

**PLUS** A £5 token to spend on anything that takes your fancy

**AND** A free copy of *The Plain English Guide*, worth £4.99

There's absolutely no risk attached to any of this - if our service is not what you're looking for we'll give you a full refund. But I believe that you'll quickly come to see us as an essential companion when it comes to choosing and buying books.

### Reviews you can trust

In putting together each issue, I try to select the books that you, the reader, will be most interested in. Not just the obvious bestsellers but the more thought-provoking, entertaining and unusual titles across the whole range of subjects - new books and classics, hardback and paperback.

I have the help of a team of independent editorial advisers and over 200 experienced reviewers. We keep a close eye on new titles and new authors and ask publishers, large and small, for review copies of those titles which look most promising. Many of

24 Seward Street, London EC1V 3GB. Great Britain   Telephone: +44 (0)171 490 9900 Fax: +44 (0)171 490 9908

*Figure 4* The Good Book Guide *direct mail letter*

the books we read end up on the reject pile. The selection we finally make for any issue of the magazine only includes titles we can genuinely recommend.

### Service you can rely on

Reviewing and recommending the best books around is only half our job. The other half is making sure that you can buy the books you *want* to buy, *when* you want to buy them.

To achieve this, we hold in our warehouse copies of every title we review, ready to despatch the moment your order reaches us. Place your order by phone, fax, e-mail or post and - almost as soon as it arrives - we'll have it ready to send to whoever you want, wherever you want, by the delivery method you want <u>and</u> we give a full replacement guarantee on *every* delivery we make.

### Not just books – videos, audios, CD-ROMS...

The range of material available on video and in other formats is growing rapidly. Some is of poor quality but there is much that is excellent. Each month we select the very best releases on video cassette - feature films, documentaries, television drama, comedy and children's titles - and we regularly offer you the best new CD-ROMs, audio tapes and music CDs.

You'll also find plenty to surprise you in the GBG Extra supplement, which each month covers a specific area in depth. Recent topics include the 17th century, Russia, Music and Christmas Gifts.

### You can order any book in print

If there's a book you want but cannot find listed in the Guide - perhaps on a subject of special interest to you - Titlefinder, our specialized book search and ordering service, will gladly find it for you.

### Satisfaction guaranteed – or your money back

I am so confident of the quality of the Guide and the reliability of our service that I am prepared to refund your subscription if you are in any way dissatisfied.

I'd also like to reassure you on one other point. We are <u>not</u> a book club. You are not obliged to order anything at all and nothing will be sent to you unless you have requested it.

### Subscribe NOW to claim your £5 token and free book

Return the enclosed invitation card today and we'll send you, by return of post, your first Good Book Guide Magazine package, together with your £5 token (which you can use towards any order for more than £20) *and* your free copy of *The Plain English Guide*. Then you'll be able to see for yourself how easy it is to track down the books you want to buy.

I look forward very much to hearing from you.

Yours sincerely

*Bonnie Falconer*

Bonnie Falconer
*Editor*

C50L

*Figure 4* The Good Book Guide *direct mail letter* (continued)

ever more evenly spread across more than 200 countries.

When we started we reviewed exclusively books. Today we review books, audio-cassettes, videos, CD-ROMs, and, once a year, a variety of gift products specifically chosen for our target audience. We have also added the Titlefinder service, which locates and supplies any book in print in the UK or US.

As far as external factors are concerned, there is now a far heavier demand on people's time and resources than there used to be. Consumers are being asked to spread finite resources across an ever widening range of subscription, membership and purchasing opportunities and, as a result, much of the international direct mail industry is experiencing a fall in response rates.

How has that affected us? The more relaxed, explanatory approach we used to take has had to become more focused, partly because the offer is now more complicated, partly because we need to shout louder to attract the same level of attention and interest.

Our primary method of subscriber recruitment direct mail has the programme pivoting around two main mailshots a year (spring and autumn). Years of testing have proved the viability of this approach, which produces 70% of our annual new subscription total. The remaining 30% are generated externally from advertising and other methods, and internally from promotions and offers to existing subscribers. Buyers are recruited through mailings of each new Catalogue to both internal and cold names, plus inserts and a variety of other methods.

To ensure that we direct our activities effectively, we constantly test and analyse everything we do. Each main mailing will always set a test pack against the latest incarnation of the control pack (we test up to 10% of the total mailing and often run smaller, ancillary tests on minor changes). All activities are carefully coded to ensure that we track every response back to a list, ad or insert specific source key and we don't settle simply for headline response rates in judging effectiveness. We have developed a sophisticated life-time value model which allows us to condense response, conversion and renewal rates and purchasing activity into a single index. This figure can then be run through a number of selection filters to give us an accurate idea of the relative effectiveness and profitability of any given recruitment activity.

Underpinning all this activity is a constant round of questioning. We seek subscriber feedback on enrolment and termination and regularly poll the entire subscriber base for views and opinions on a wide range of subjects and aspects of our service. This year, as part of an ongoing programme tracking the growth and development of the CD-ROM market, we sent a detailed questionnaire probing current activity and future intent to every subscriber who has ever purchased a CD-ROM from us.

This information is fed into a response analysis programme we've developed in conjunction with our mailing house which deselects names with low propensities to respond and to spend, based on a number of carefully identified selection criteria. This live and dead zone analysis has yielded substantial improvements in list performance and yield (we know because we constantly test the dead zone as well as working the live zone).

This certainly gives the feel of what is necessary to implement direct mail successfully on any scale. It links with planning and research; and will not work without clarity of purpose and a sound base of information. Clearly good direct mail (or good anything else) does not just happen. The kind of thinking demonstrated here is important (and not only valid in terms of direct mail; a similarly thorough approach would strengthen any promotional campaign). But the potential is clear too. It is a technique that seems set to be used much more in business in the future.

So, with this in mind, you may like to look more carefully at the next mailshot you receive. Across industry the best represents the 'high-tech' end of advertising, and while many talk of 'junk-mail', many more buy and buy again. Certain areas of business use this technique extensively; others little or not at all – another area perhaps for more experiment and development.

Direct mail is subject to the *detail* of what is done; something as simple as a different headline may significantly affect response. It has many virtues as a promotional method – not least the fact that it can be tested (a small shot may be sent to judge its effectiveness before more money is spent circulating it widely) – and is likely to play an increasingly important part in the promotion mix of many organisations in future.

---

**Warning**

Direct mail, certainly in its less complex forms, may seem easy – just write a letter, get together a brochure and get underway. This is misleading. The intention in the description given here is to emphasise the need for attention to detail. An ill-thought-out mailing may produce nothing and be very costly. For all its potential strengths, it is a technique that must be used with care and, where possible, with expertise.

---

**Definition:** *Direct marketing*

Direct marketing includes direct mail, and is sometimes cast as direct-response marketing. Things other than mail shots work in the same way. For example, direct-response advertisements in newspapers and magazines (and even TV shopping these days) work on a similar basis. The message must be complete and persuasive, allowing action – whether ordering or some other procedure – to be taken without further information.

Direct marketing is the umbrella term for this whole area; the methods for making it work are, in principle, the same as for direct mail (see DIRECT MAIL).

# Display and merchandising

**Introduction**

The application of display and merchandising is wide. It has relevance in industrial and business-to-business marketing, for example in showrooms. But here we will investigate it in its main context, linked to retailing.

Merchandising is the term given to the promotional effect of how layout and display are arranged in retail outlets of all sorts. Have a look around next time you go shopping. Are there shops with window displays that make you want to look inside? Do you notice, in a supermarket, that essentials, such as bread or sugar, are very often at the back of the store? This means that customers have to pass many other, less essential, items en route to those they really want to buy. The word 'impulse buy' is used to describe purchases made on the spur of the moment because something catches the eye. This is not a way of making people buy something they do not want, so much as a way of making sure they buy sooner, rather than later and from somewhere else. So, items likely to attract people in get prime display; essential items go at the back.

Merchandising and display have clear objectives. Research confirms they are a key influence on purchasing decisions. They are designed to:

1. *Sell more*: Sell a quantity over and above the level that would occur if no action were taken; some people will always want certain products and search them out.
2. *Inform*: Tell the customer about numbers of matters in various ways: they tell them a shop is there; they indicate something of the range of products it sells; they highlight what is new; they direct people to the right section of the shop, and so on.
3. *Persuade*: Make the message attractive, understandable and convincing – it is this aspect that can prompt the action that is really wanted: a sale!

They have to put over messages to many different groups of people, in particular to:

- those who may pass the shop by, who will not even enter unless something external catches their eye

- the ubiquitous 'browser' and those who come into the shop for one small item but may buy more; this is one reason most shops sell a mixture of things – to maximise the number of people they attract
- those who are active or regular customers.

The general effects here are important. Of course, there are all sorts of people within each category: young, old, rich, poor, male, female, and so on. Because of their different intentions some messages will be general; others will be specific, aimed exclusively at one group or another. In addition, there are the products themselves. To say the promotional and display permutations become numerous is an understatement; in many shops – certainly supermarkets – the number of lines stocked is numbered in thousands.

Any change of products to be sold (and therefore displayed), coupled with customers' tendency to notice only what is new, means displays must be changed or updated regularly. Displays are there, in part, to remind and to freshen the interest. If you consider your own high street, you may notice a window display instantly if it is eye-catching (you may even go into the shop and buy something); however, if the window is never changed, it becomes part of the scenery and, after a while, makes no impression.

Display, therefore, must be carefully carried out to achieve the right effect. The mnemonic AIDA demonstrates exactly what needs to be done in this and other promotional contexts:

**A** – catch the customers' *attention*

**I** – arouse their *interest*

**D** – turn their interest into *desire*

**A** – prompt *action*.

To take a simple example, a customer seeing a display of books labelled 'for holiday reading', is attracted by perhaps one aspect of the display – a bucket and spade – and moves from:

'What's this?' to
'Perhaps I do need a book for my holiday' to
'That looks just the thing' to
'I'll buy it'.

This is the essential principle behind good display, and checking a particular display to see if it will carry customers through this kind of sequence is a useful test of its likely effectiveness. So too are ringing the changes and surprising customers. All sorts of interesting combinations are possible.

## Shop layout

It is beyond the scope of this book to consider the physical layout of a shop in detail. In any case, many aspects are fixed, for a variety of reasons: cost, the lease will not allow change, etc. Others are not, and certain basic principles of layout are therefore worth commenting on briefly as follows:

1. *Traffic flow*: 90 per cent of the population are right-handed and will turn accordingly on entering a shop and go round it clockwise. (This is compounded by habit as so many supermarkets and department stores recognise and encourage it.)

2. *Eyes*: Customers select most readily from goods displayed at eye level (60–62 inches for women, a little higher for men). This puts very high or low shelves at a corresponding disadvantage; and many shops have plenty of both in order to maximise use of space. There are problems here with the volume of stock to be carried and displayed, but customers may resent having to shop on their hands and knees. Manufacturers must spend part of their promotion and sales effort on securing space in prime locations for their products.

3. *Quantity*: Customers buy more readily from things displayed in quantity, rather than a single example of a product – hence the piles of goods characteristic of many retailers.

4. *Vertical display*: Products displayed together are found more manageable if they are above and below each other, rather than arranged side by side.

5. *Accident*: Customers are less likely to browse among or pick up a product from any display that appears precarious, e.g. if they think they may not be able to balance an item back in position or that other items may fall, especially if they fear damaging something fragile or valuable. This is important because in certain shops the customer needs to pick up and inspect the product; indeed he or she may not be prepared to buy without doing so.

6. *Choice*: Customers are attuned to choice. A number of options make this easy to exercise; products sell better from within a range of similar items.

7. *Relationships*: Customers expect to find related items close at hand (e.g. pens, pencils and paper go naturally together; something like strawberries and cream might seem to fit in different areas – fruit and dairy products – but will sell well together).

8. *Cash points (tills)*: These need to be convenient and clearly indicated (and, of course, promptly and helpfully staffed; but that is another issue) and can be a focal point for some display.

9. *Position*: In a large shop, people will walk or search for things they feel

are essential (as already discussed it is no accident that bread and sugar are normally at the rear of the supermarket). If children's toys are up three flights of stairs, parents with pushchairs will not make that shop first choice.

10. *Colour*: This has a fashion, and an image, connotation – bright may be seen as brash – so it must be carefully chosen. This applies to display materials, e.g. a backcloth in the window, as well as to decoration. If colour is too dull, however, it is not noticed.

11. *Lighting*: This must be good, especially where it is important to see the colour of a product clearly; if something cannot be found or seen clearly no one will buy it, and people's patience is limited.

12. *Seating*: Some shops actively encourage browsing so, if lack of space does not prohibit, they provide chairs or perhaps a stool near the till for older customers.

13. *Background music*: This evokes strong opinions: some like it, some hate it. However, the reverse, a library-like silence, can also be off-putting. Certainly, careful choice of music and awareness of volume level are necessary. Some shops favour relaxing, predominantly classical and soft jazz, music which may become very much part of their overall style. Others, particularly those catering for a young age group, go for a brasher approach.

14. *Character*: Part of the overall atmosphere will come from the main physical elements of the shop; dark wooden panelling has quite a different feel from more modern alternatives (both have their place).

15. *Floor*: This will be noticed; is it quiet to walk on? can it be kept clean easily? does it (or should it) direct customer flow, using different colours for pathways?

16. *Reach*: If things are out of reach, people are reluctant to 'be a nuisance' by asking and they therefore may not buy.

17. *Signing*: As people are reluctant to ask, there must be enough clear signs to direct people easily to everything in the shop. Many signs are virtually in-store advertisements and these can be used to good effect; they must be clear, but can also be used creatively. This is another area where simple ideas and variety can be useful. With control of image in mind some retailers go their own way – Dixons, for example, only have their own signs, posters, etc. in their stores; others take and use material from their suppliers (another aspect of marketing is to make what is offered attractive and desirable).

18. *Standing space*: Space to stand and look without completely blocking 'traffic' flow may encourage purchase; this links to cost, with lower-rental, out-of-town shops probably having more space to play with.

19. *Security*: Last, but by no means least, this is sadly important in every

aspect of retailing. Visibility of, for example, closed circuit TV is important. So too is simple vigilance. Retailing is rarely sufficiently profitable to sustain a high level of pilfering without concern.

This list is not, of course, comprehensive but these factors are important; the overall physical construction and layout is the backcloth to any display, both in the shop and in the window. Merchandising perhaps demonstrates the need to leave no 'promotional corner' ineffective.

# Distribution

**Introduction**

Marketing must link to the market, not just in terms of having a focus on customers and their needs, but literally. Goods and services have to be brought to market and direct contact created with buyers. Distribution is what allows this to happen.

Let us take general principles first. However good any product or service, however well promoted and however much customers – and potential customers – want it, it has to be put into a position which allows customers easy access; it must be distributed. And this can be a complex business, though it is certainly a marketing variable, albeit one that many regard as rather more fixed than, in fact, it is. Consider the variety of ways in which goods are made available. Consumer products are sold in shops – retailers – but these may vary enormously in nature, from supermarkets and department stores, to specialist retailers, general stores and even market traders. These may, in turn, be variously located: in a town or city centre, in an out-of-town shopping area, in a multi-storey shopping centre, or on a neighbourhood corner site.

But the complexity does not stop there. Retailers may be supplied by a network of wholesalers or distributors, or they may simply not be involved; some consumer products are sold by mail order, or door to door, or through home parties (like Tupperware). A similar situation applies to services, with even traditional banking services being made available in stores, from machines in the street and by post and telephone – even on a drive-in basis. Banking also illustrates the changes going on in the area of distribution, with many of these developments being comparatively recent moves away from solely traditional branch operations. Business-to-business industrial products are similarly complex in the range of distributive options they use.

Areas where change has occurred, or is occurring, can prompt rapid customer reaction if the new means offered are found to be convenient. Old habits may die hard, but if change is made attractive and visible then new practices can be established and quickly become the norm. Conversely, if distribution method is inconvenient for customers then they will seek other ways of access to the product (or simply not buy it). Sometimes though, inconveniences are tolerated because need is high or compensated for by other factors. For example, some customers will put up with queues in one shop only because the alternative is too far away, or has no convenient parking.

How a company analyses the distributive possibilities and uses a chosen method or methods effectively is certainly important to overall marketing success. Such analysis can be facilitated by 'market mapping', a process which looks graphically at the range of options and the different routes either available or in operation (see MARKET MAPPING).

There are a number of good reasons for delegating what is an essential element of the marketing mix. For example:

- Distributive intermediaries provide a ready-made network of contacts that would otherwise take years to establish at what might be a prohibitive cost; clearly even a large company might balk at the thought of setting up its own chain of specialist shops, and the incidence of this is very low.
- Distributors are objective and are not tied to one product. They can offer a range that appeals to their customers, electing to pitch this wide, or narrow (and there are some shops which sell very narrow ranges, e.g. ties, books on sport, coffee, etc.).
- Distributors provide an environment that the customer needs in order to make a choice. If a customer wants to compare competing brands, this can be done conveniently in the store. If a distributor stocks a product, and is well known and has a positive image, this may by association enhance the overall attractiveness of the experience to the consumer. Allowing potential customers to view a wide choice – as in, say, selecting a television set – is an important aspect of encouraging sales.
- Distributors can spread the costs of stocking and selling one product over all the items they carry, thereby distributing it at a lower cost than a supplier operating alone.
- The cost of bad debts is sometimes lower than it would otherwise be, as the distributor effectively shares the risk.
- Since the distributor is rewarded by a discount off the selling price, no capital is tied up in holding local stocks, though overlong credit can (does?) dilute this effect.
- Distributors have, or should have, good specialist knowledge of retailing or distribution, which the principal may not possess; this clearly varies across different kinds of retailer.

So far so good, but there can be conflicts of interest between principals and distributors since:

- Distributors are not as committed to a particular product as its producer is. If the customer prefers another, the distributor will substitute it. If a customer asks for advice – 'I want to arrange a weekend break and I see there are some good deals in France' – that customer is just as likely to end up going to the Channel Isles, unless the agent has a particular reason to sell one destination rather than another. In some cases discount structures may lead agents to make particular recommendations that benefit them.

- Distributors may use the manufacturer's product for their own promotional purposes, and this is often linked to price cutting; not every manufacturer wants the price of a particular product cut (a manufacturer may feel it dilutes image, but be powerless to stop it being done).

- They may drop the product from their list if they believe they can make a better profit with another line; this will clearly affect directly competing lines.

- Many distributors expect the manufacturer to stimulate demand for the product; for example by advertising or providing display material. Sometimes they are more interested in the support than in the product itself.

- Many are tough on terms (draconian is a word one hears regularly from some suppliers!) and have complex ordering procedures. At the same time they distance themselves from collaboration that could perhaps increase sales for both parties (with chains, significant decisions are 'made at HQ' and sales representatives may be left dealing in individual stores with young, inexperienced staff who do not know whether it is Tuesday or Breakfast). I exaggerate a little, I hasten to add.

The question of whether a company deals direct with the consumer is, therefore, dependent upon two things. First upon the availability of suitable channels and the company's willingness to include additional products in the range it sells. Secondly, on balancing the economies of the distributors' lower selling and servicing costs with the disadvantages of not being present at the point where customers make decisions, and thus having less control over the selling process. Realistically, many companies have no option but to go through existing channels (whether these involve shops or not), though exactly how this is done and the mix involved can be varied. In addition, more radical variants may need to be found and run alongside (and without alienating) the retail chain; this can certainly be a way of increasing business.

## What channel of distribution to choose

Although this is, as we have seen already, a decision involving some complex, interlocking issues, six main factors will influence the route taken:

1. *Customer characteristics*: Distributors are generally required when customers are widely dispersed, there is a large number of them and they buy frequently in small amounts. This is certainly true of many sectors of every-day product, less so or not at all with regard to more specialist items.

2. *Product characteristics*: Direct distribution is required when bulky or heavy products are involved. Bulky products need channel arrangements that minimise the shipping distance and the number of handlings; even a brief look at physical distribution costs shows the importance of this factor.

   Where high unit value can cover higher unit selling costs, then any manufacturer can keep control over distribution by dealing direct; as with certain off-the-page distribution systems or, at the far end of the spectrum, those who sell door-to-door. Finally, products requiring installation or maintenance are generally sold through a limited network, such as sole agents.

3. *Distributor characteristics*: Distributors are more useful when their skills of low-cost contact, service and storage are more important than their lack of commitment to one product or brand. If very specific support is necessary then other options may be preferred.

4. *Competitive characteristics*: The channels chosen may often be influenced by the channels competitors use, and there may be dangers in moving away too far and too fast from what a market expects and likes. The competitive interaction in this way between retailers is another variable. In the area of fast food, Burger King try to obtain sites near to McDonald's; on the other hand, some manufacturers, such as Avon Cosmetics, choose not to compete for scarce positions in retail stores and have established profitable door-to-door direct-selling operations instead. Similarly, major chains may seek to open branches near existing smaller, independent, retailers, not only to take advantage of their market knowledge – they are in an area where there is a demand – but with the aim of replacing them all together. This last may well not be entirely in customers' interests and illustrates one aspect of the sheer power of major retailing groups.

5. *Company characteristics*: The size of a company often correlates with its market share. The bigger its market share, the easier it is to find distributors willing to handle the product – thus even a small shop is

likely to find a corner for major brands, and will be selective about what else it stocks. It may not be able to stock everything, but will find space for anything it believes in. Where there is clearly profit to be made no-one wants to miss out on it. Similarly, a supplier may be innovative (and/or build on a strength) and seek ways of becoming less dependent on the normal chain of distribution.

Creativity may have a role to play here. For instance, cosmetics may sell well in outlets that simply display them, but a store putting on make-up demonstrations (or letting the manufacturer do so) may create an edge, at least for a while.

Additionally, a policy of fast delivery is less compatible with a large number of stages in the channel and there is a danger that slow delivery (measured in market terms) dilutes marketing effectiveness. As service standards increase so there is less room for anyone who lags behind to do as well as they might – slow delivery is increasingly not tolerated.

6. *Environmental characteristics*: Changes in the economic and legal environment can also bring about changes in distributive structures. For example, when the market is depressed, manufacturers want to move their goods to market in the most economic way. They thus cut out intermediaries or non-essential services to compete on price and deal direct. Again, legal restrictions have been introduced in the UK in recent years to prevent channel characteristics which may weaken competition.

Overall trends within retailing also influence how things are done. Out-of-town shopping, the use of the car (or restrictions on it), and everything from the rental cost to the desirability of an area all influence the likelihood of shoppers patronising a particular area, and thus a particular shop. Certainly this may influence where all sorts of product are bought, and this in turn may influence what is bought.

An example might be the development of Covent Garden market in London. Now an attractive area of restaurants and entertainment as well as shops, it attracts people from far and wide. Someone might well buy something, a present perhaps, in a shop there, choosing something different from what they might have bought if they had shopped somewhere else. Such decisions are based on what is there, how it is displayed and more.

A major retailing trend is towards out-of-town shopping centres of various sorts. In some, small, independent shops fit in well; in others, groups of the big retail groups (Sainsburys, Dixons, etc.) predominate and the environment is not right for the small shopkeeper.

The bigger the environmental change the more likely it is to have repercussions. And there are doubtless many changes still to come in this area.

Usually it is possible to identify several different types of channel or distributor. In certain industries some of the alternatives may be further from standard practice than others, but that does not mean they are not worthy of consideration, or cannot be part of the distribution mix. Things that are normal now may have originally been difficult to establish. For example, many in business know and deal with Wyvern Books who sell business titles, like this one, by direct mail, sending tiny cards in packs of 20–30 in one envelope. This way of selling had not been done before and, at the outset, was viewed with scepticism by some of those involved. Not only does the system work well, but the number of cards included in one 'shot' has grown since its inception, and so has the number of sales.

Some companies are, of course, bound to the standard form in their field, but the point here is that it pays to remain open minded; channels may change little, traditional routes may remain the most important as they create the greatest volume of business, but other possibilities may still create some growth.

There are still without doubt many innovative ways of distribution in prospect (the internet, to name but one of current interest) and things that seem unlikely today will no doubt be viewed as entirely normal in years to come. We all have 20/20 hindsight. The trick for suppliers is to make sure some marketing time, effort and thinking goes into exploring and testing new methods. This is, of course, true of most things, but distribution is a prime candidate for the very reason that many do see it as essentially static, at least in the short term. Perhaps this just means there is all the more possibility of using it to steal an edge over more conservative competitors.

So, alternatives need be explored to see which channel or combination of channels best meets the firm's objectives and constraints. However, the best choice of channel must take into account the degree to which the company can control, or at least influence, the distribution channel created.

In some fields, for example foods, many suppliers may feel that they are too much at the beck and call of the retailers, especially the large ones. Large customers need careful handling: they are not just different in size, they are different in nature (See KEY ACCOUNTS).

## Distribution management

Not only are chosen distributors likely to work better on behalf of any manufacturer if communications, support (e.g. information, training and service) and motivation are good, but they will have their own ideas, and a good working relationship must be adopted if both are to profit from the partnership. At best, all this takes time, and it is often easy simply to see people as suppliers, rather than someone to work with. Yet the best may only be obtained from a market when the two parties do work, and work effectively, together.

Distribution is a key element in marketing, one that sometimes goes by default because existing methods are regarded as fixed, but one where making existing arrangements work well – and seeking new or additional ones – can create further sales success.

Distribution is a vital process that links the company to its customers, and thus marketing activity can be made or broken by its performance. It is essential that the right methods are chosen and that everyone down the line is worked with effectively. Among retailers, few will even consider taking on a new product (or taking on board any idea) unless they can be convinced that the demand exists and is more that an optimistic gleam in a supplier's eye. They need to know which market segment the product is aimed at and whether it fits with their customer franchise.

Working through any channel of distribution demands clear policy: that all parties have clear, understood and agreed expectations of each other; that terms of trade (discounts and all financial arrangements) are equally understood and agreed; that sufficient time and resources are put into the on-going process of managing, communicating with and motivating those organisations and people upon whom sales are ultimately dependent. There is always a range of options. Some are seen as 'the norm', others as peripheral or 'unlikely to work', still more we can as yet not anticipate. But whatever is done, whatever range of ways may be used together, the distribution process is an area that marketing must aim to influence. It is at the interface, whatever form that takes, that sales are ultimately made. So the supplier must work effectively with what is necessarily a given (and this includes dealing with aspects of the business that you would rather were different), and also seek new approaches and methods where appropriate and take an innovative and creative approach to the whole process of distribution.

# *Exhibitions*

**Introduction**

Exhibitions are hard work. Not least they are hard on the feet and sometimes the stomach. This may well be as true for those who visit them as those who organise and exhibit at them. Nevertheless, many take place and many people make use of them; they are an important marketing technique and worth some comment.

If there is a very tight budget then major exhibitions may be ruled out, though some companies get round this by sharing a stand, working with others who are non-competitive. But the range of events coming under the exhibition heading is substantial, and includes many smaller, local, events from country shows and fairs to events put on by local chambers of trade. Even a village fête may be an opportunity for a small stand, and the author knows of one company selling dried flower arrangements for which the latter is a regularly successful activity. What matters is not simply the overall costs, which are always important, but also the cost per enquiry or per order.

Every exhibition possibility must be looked at in a very hard-nosed way. Exhibition organisers will always tend to say their show is right for you, indeed those selling exhibition space can be 'pushy'. Each possible event needs checking out. Once a decision is made to participate, what you get from it will be in direct proportion to the way in which you undertake it. So here we review the principles of successful exhibiting. These involve factors which are perhaps best described as promotional, but which also overlap into selling techniques (see PROMOTION and SALES FORCE AND SELLING). By getting into some detail here the personal nature of some promotional techniques is well illustrated.

Exhibitions produce a unique environment. There are many of them (the Exhibition Industry Federation describes it as an industry worth more than £1.5 billion) and, because of the scale of the exhibitions industry, a good deal of research exists about them. The following points are all research-based:

1.  Attendees are receptive to what exhibitors have to sell. They have given

up time to check out specific areas and there are none of the usual distractions of the office, such as phones, interruptions, etc.

2. The cost of a lead generated at an exhibition is low (certainly compared to salespeople's time) and requires, on average, less follow-up contact to convert.

3. Exhibitions provide a quality audience. The great majority of visitors have buying influence: more than half are middle management and above. Special categories are useful too; for example, a third of those visiting exhibitions are new to their job, needing to check things out fast and looking actively for new suppliers.

4. The average visitor spends five hours at an exhibition and, in addition to seeking new contacts, spends much of the time talking to people he or she knows (so it is a good way of maintaining contact with existing customers).

In addition, exhibitions are, of course, interactive. Products can be touched and tried and demonstrations watched. Feedback is immediately available, and progress towards a decision can be certain and fast. Furthermore, many exhibitions are specialist and the fastest-growing section is that where exhibitors are all from one industry.


## Dangers and opportunities

Of course, there are dangers and it is certainly possible to exhibit for the wrong reasons: because competitors are there; because customers expect it; to entertain. But there are also opportunities and there are certainly many reasons for exhibiting. These need not be mutually exclusive, but need thinking through if everything is to be considered and arrangements made to achieve everything intended. Intentions may include, for example:

- to take direct orders on the stand
- to demonstrate something
- to provide information (and get information about competitors)
- to find names/contacts for long-term conversion
- to meet/entertain agents or distributors
- to achieve public relations and press coverage
- to introduce or test a new product or promotion
- to do market research.

Whatever the reasons, they should be reviewed and agreed before the event. Some may be mutually incompatible: for instance, salespeople will have less time to take orders if they are completing lengthy research questionnaires with prospects. All need to be specifically reflected in the organisation and arrangements.

There also need to be clear *sales objectives*. These may not always be simply to take orders, but can also usefully include:

- arranging a trial
- arranging a demonstration at their premises or yours
- agreeing/arranging a further meeting
- discussing details to allow a quotation/proposal/survey to follow.

Whatever the reasons generally, and whatever the specific sales objectives, the activity is people-intensive and questions need to be asked regarding who will attend and take part – sales, service, technical, export, management and so on – and also who will remain to 'mind the shop'.

Setting clear objectives is the first task when considering exhibiting. With clear objectives in mind preparations – important here as with all successfully implemented promotion – can commence in earnest.

## Preparation

This must be systematic and thorough. There will be 101 details to check, from the necessary product samples to making sure you pack the coffee mugs (remember nothing or virtually nothing will be provided by the organiser). I asked Susan Cline of Design Consultancy Services in London, who has much experience of the process, how it should be approached. She quoted three key preliminary areas that should be assessed by all potential exhibitors before making a decision to exhibit:

1. *The exhibition*: Will it attract the type of visitor who could become your client? Will some of your existing clients go there? Will there be enough visitors to make it worth your while? What about the exhibitors? They are as important as the visitors. A company is known by the company it keeps. How many exhibitors will there be? What kind of companies will be represented? Will your closest competitors and rivals be there? If so, can you afford not to show your face?
2. *The timing*: The timing of the show is very important. Will you have suitable staff who can devote time to being on the stand? Watch out for conflicting commitments such as delivery or production dates.
3. *The cost*: The rent for the stand and the cost of having it constructed and dressed are only the most obvious elements. There are other expenses to take into account. Remember to include the cost of travel, food and accommodation for staff, and the cost of drinks and hospitality for clients.

## Implementing a decision to exhibit

First, a good relationship is needed with the organiser. Have a named contact for the organiser to work with. Make sure that he or she knows what you need; the company must speak with one voice.

Through that contact make sure that the position of the stand is suitable. Is it within a group of similar services or merchandise and not isolated among unrelated stands? It may be possible to negotiate a better position (or even a better deal) with the organiser if you have taken trouble from the start to establish a good working relationship.

Find out from the organisers what services they supply to exhibitors for each stand. For example, will they arrange for lighting and furniture to be supplied as part of the basic package? Or will that involve extra expense? What opportunities are there for free publicity or linked publicity as part of the overall exhibition arrangements?

An exhibitor does not want all visitors to be chance ones. It is an opportunity to meet with existing customers, to catch up with dormant ones, and for an extra contact with others who have yet to be persuaded to spare time for real discussions. Such people need to be invited to attend.

Presentation on the day is of the utmost importance. A stand must communicate a clear and simple message, making sure that the image presented by the stand represents the company's best face. Make it welcoming. Do not create any barrier that might seem daunting for a visitor to cross – no physical barrier, no design barrier and no psychological barrier. It can be helpful to have something of particular interest near the front of the stand. Then visitors can approach it without feeling that they are encroaching on your territory and without worrying that some over-zealous salesperson will pounce on them. All this needs pre-planning.

Staff briefing, and perhaps training for exhibition work, are essential. Everyone who serves on the stand must appear competent, alert and interested. Make sure they each have a job to do and they each have targets to aim for, and think about this well before the event.

All this, and more, must be geared to the overall effect that the stand seeks to have. The key intention should be not simply to be visible (however smart or professional that visibility is) but to make that visibility link to a truly persuasive presence.

## Exhibiting persuasiveness

The stand is not simply a static advertisement. The whole point of exhibiting is to meet people; they need to be encouraged on to the stand

and persuaded towards your objectives. Consider some of the many reasons why people visit exhibitions; they come not only to do business and place orders, but also to:

- set up a future appointment
- see a demonstration
- deal with specific technical queries
- negotiate the best terms
- see new products/ideas
- find answers to a problem
- take a decision to purchase
- compare the range of competitors
- collect information for the future
- test/try products.

All these need handling in different ways, and so may necessitate deploying a range of differing skills. The person who runs the best demonstration, for instance, may not be the best negotiator.

Other people attend too, and visit your stand. These include your competitors, professional literature collectors, drink scroungers and other time-wasters, as well as some of your own customers – there perhaps for a reason preferably not to be dealt with publicly at an exhibition, such as a complaint about discounts. The good exhibitor can spot such people at twenty paces, indeed doing so is an ability that should be cultivated, together with the ability to handle people in this strange environment. Rarely, in any other way, can a customer talk to three potential suppliers in the same hour; they take full advantage of this, but they do also regard it as a 'day out'. They expect to be treated well, and all expect you to deal with them individually as if they were the only visitor to the exhibition, or at least to your stand. It may be the only time they meet on 'the supplier's patch', and the encounter must make a lasting and positive impression. For those who know a supplier less well (or not at all), they must find a welcoming front and not find the show, or the stand in particular, daunting.

Persuasive techniques must be used at every stage of the contact.

*Note:* *The techniques of making face-to-face meetings persuasive are reviewed, in detail, in the section* SALES FORCE AND SELLING. *Here we look solely at certain issues which are specific to the exhibition scene.*

The first step is to encourage those moving through the exhibition on to the stand. People can be actively put off by both the stand and those manning it. So avoid:

- obstructing gangways/entrances
- salespeople lining up and appearing as a barrier

- staff gathering in groups, talking together
- leaving parts of the stand unattended
- any clutter such as files, bags, coats, used coffee cups, untidy tables, full ashtrays, etc.
- the 'cosy, do not disturb' look, with staff sitting around on all available seats
- people looking bored, aggressive, defensive, tired
- staff being *too* eager to get someone on to the stand
- high pressure 'pouncing'.

Make sure the stand is clean, accessible, open, well-lit, interesting, neither too crowded nor too empty and has clear spaces, an element of movement, something going on (a video, a demonstration), a clear enquiry point, literature available – and accessible, smart, welcoming staff (identified by badges or uniforms). It is vital that visitors can easily:

- see the product
- read displays
- find and take literature
- watch anything going on
- ask questions
- prompt more detailed discussions.

Everything about the set-up must make it easy and welcoming for people to come on to the stand; every detail counts.

The next step is to establish contact.

## Taking the initiative

Nobody, but nobody, should *ever* say 'Can I help you?' (to which most say, instinctively, 'No thank you') but everyone on the stand should be prepared to take a positive and appropriate initiative. It is just as off-putting as 'Can I help you?' for staff to launch into a long, technical explanation replete with jargon. If a start is made with a question, it must be an *open* question, in other words something which does not lend itself to being answered by 'Yes' or 'No' (this is the problem with the hackneyed 'Can I help you?').

So, something like:

- 'What are you hoping to find at the show?'
- 'How much do you know about us?'
- 'Where are you from?'

which demand a fuller reply, tend to do better. Equally, the approach must not frighten people off. There are probably people jumping out at them every few yards, so remember the purpose of this first initiative is to:

- make the visitor feel at ease
- get them talking
- discover their exact interest
- identify their needs
- get them deciding is it *worth* spending some time on the stand.

So, try to start with unchallenging openings:

- introduce yourself by name (this can often result in the visitor giving you their name in return)
- offer a quick demonstration or video explanation of the point attracting attention
- discuss their particular point of interest or need
- ask general questions to open the conversation, e.g. 'What do you use (product) for?' 'When might you be considering upgrading?'

continuing to favour open questions as you do so. The overall aim is to move effortlessly into a relaxed and interesting conversation, not to 'hassle' people.

Once such a conversation is under way the next key stage is the best identification of individual needs. At this point the approach must be tailored towards the kind of person that has come on to the stand – an existing or dormant customer, a prospect, someone 'just looking', a competitor – with more specific questions leading the way. Not every visitor will be worth time and attention, but once you establish that the person is not a real prospect, then always handle them politely and professionally (remember, they may become a future customer, or will know a potential customer – or be useful in some other way).

If they require information or assistance, give it to them quickly and politely, but do not waste time if the stand is busy. If the stand is quiet, a 'just looking' visitor can be valuable – a stand with people already on it and talking tends to encourage others to stop and look.

It is important to remember that not everyone has the inclination, or the time, to talk to you on the day. But they are presumably involved in the topic of the event, and it may be worth following them up either specifically and individually or, at the least, adding them to a mailing list. So, one of the prime jobs at exhibitions is to collect names; but how do you get these names? The classic way is to have a goldfish-type bowl for people to drop business cards into, though you may need to give them a reason to do so. A draw, with a prize, often in the form of product (which is cheapest) seems to work well. Do think about prizes, however. A bottle of champagne may be nice, but is a bit hackneyed and yet, unless you are a travel agent, a fortnight in the Bahamas is costly to provide. Swopping products works well. Team up with another (non-competitive) exhibitor and let them give something you provide as a prize and vice versa; this will make both stands look more creative. Anything that can be added to this sort of technique in order to get more from it should be built in:

- run a draw every day (not just at the end of the exhibition)
- announce the time of the draw
- get someone well known to do it
- announce the winner(s) in a press release, notice, etc.
- if the prize is an 'event' (e.g. a flight in a hot air balloon) report on that later

and follow it up by keeping in touch with the winner(s). If cost is a big factor it may be better to have one memorable, noticeable, prize rather than several routine ones.

Finally, keep an eye on those who deposit cards. The author once saw an exhibition visitor deposit a whole box of cards in the bowl in an attempt to raise the odds of winning an attractive prize. Some cards are deposited at just the right moment to engage the visitor in conversation.


## What next?

One of the most critical areas of exhibiting happens after the event; and that is follow-up action. Too often people visit a stand, express interest, leave a business card, are promised a later contact – but never hear another word. This negates all the effort – time and money – that has gone into being there and is neither good public relations nor good selling.

It must *always* be the case that every encounter on the stand prompts certain specific actions, so whoever meets the customer must remember:

- to give their business card to every visitor
- that every visitor's name, company, address and telephone number should be recorded
- that outline details of the enquiry should be noted
- that promised action must be highlighted and implemented
- if action is to be taken by someone not present at the show, that allocation must be made and details passed on
- if there is any delay, an acknowledgement letter should be sent to the customer (these should be ready *before* the event, at least in outline – they may need personalising).

Not only should such records be used to prompt and record further action

– it may, after all, take several contacts or a number of meetings to tie down firm business – but it should be used to analyse the results in the longer term. How many leads were there? How many were converted to business? After how long? At what cost? What other contacts were made? Were any public relations activities possible – and useful? These, and other, questions need asking and answering. All being well, there will be a general sense of euphoria after the exhibition. It went well. The stand did not fall down. The drinks budget was not exceeded. And there were many visitors, all expressing interest and pleasure at being there. Such a feeling must be borne out by the facts. With an eye on the budget a decision must be made as to whether this may, or may not, be an exhibition to attend in future. The record of achievement will help plan future actions.

So, what – specifically – should be analysed? It will depend on the type of business involved. It should include internal and external factors, and is worth thinking through to produce a comprehensive list that suits the specific case.

The following is representative of the sort of factors involved:

1. How many prospect names were collected?
2. How many specific enquiries received? (Or requests for quotes or any other interim stage?)
3. How many follow-up meetings were fixed?
4. How much actual business (orders) was done?
5. How well were objectives achieved?
6. How well did all the arrangements go?

And, of course, what thoughts are there about what to do differently next time?

This post-exhibition analysis is potentially very useful. The exhibition itself will produce a busy period, preparing for it and running it. Immediately afterwards, with follow-up activity to implement and everything that has been going on 'back at the ranch' to catch up on, it is all too easy to neglect this analysis. A series of exhibitions that build on the experience of past ones will be much more valuable in the long term. It is a prime method of contacting large numbers of people in a short period of time. If it suits, it can be a very valuable technique.

Finally, a reminder that not the only options in this area are major events, which may be too expensive for some. It is worth a systematic review of what is available (geographically or otherwise). Check local:

• press (including business publications)
• Chambers of Commerce or Trade
• societies (including local branches of national bodies)

and keep your eyes open for everything that is run that might provide a platform.

Exhibitions demonstrate marketing in action in microcosm. They involve analysis and planning, demand a creative approach and ultimately are only made effective by the way the people aspect of what goes on works. A visit to one can give you an opportunity to observe how marketing works (or does not!); being an exhibitor means utilising many marketing and sales skills.

**Definition:** *Exporting*

See OVERSEAS MARKETING.

# *External environment*

**Introduction**

Here we review external factors affecting the marketing system: what are sometimes referred to as 'environmental' factors, including a particularly important one – competition.

The whole marketing system has to operate in an environment which restricts it, or actively works against it. Such restrictions include:

- total demand
- availability of capital and labour
- competition (including worldwide competition)
- legal requirements
- supply of raw materials
- channels of distribution – e.g. retail power and practice, overseas agents and conditions.

The first two are clearly restrictions. If vanishingly few people want, say, a magazine about Etruscan archaeology, then it is pointless to assume demand justifies a massive print run – however worthy the volume in question may be. Similarly, unless financial resources are up to the job, development plans of whatever sort may need to be paced. And labour, in the terms we mean here, indicates the availability of specific expertise, so, for example, without the public relations capacity and skill that will get a product talked about, it is no good seeing such a PR effect as the main plank of its promotional strategy.

## Broad competition

Any such restrictions must be carefully considered, because of their effect on the business. For instance, competition is easy to recognise as a restriction. Few companies are monopolies (and if they are many governments will try to stop that situation continuing – or starting, in the case of mergers) but what is competition? Other companies making and selling the same product? Yes, but it is more than this.

Take the example of a pen, say a middle range ballpoint. It obviously competes with other similar products, but also to a degree with higher quality pens, fountain pens and thus with rollerball or fibre 'nibs', and with pencils. And what about word processors or personal organisers whose use reduces the need to write? It goes further: many pens are given as gifts, so that puts them in competition with CDs, books, perfume and . . . the ubiquitous socks, etc.

This broad effect is always present and needs to be kept in mind by marketers. Consumers have plenty of choice, especially regarding 'discretionary spending' (that done after the purchase of essentials). Does someone change the car, book an exotic holiday or paint the outside of the house? Do they go to a movie, hire a video . . . or have an early night? All options, involving major or minor expenditure, involve such wide choices – and this is long before the stage where, having decided on the car, the decision of which particular one has to be made.

Restriction means just that. Some factors are at least bound up with the business and are comparatively easy to work with. The lack of an overseas distributor in, say, Malaysia may hamper a firm's export, but it is easily recognisable and action can, potentially, be taken to correct the situation, given a little time.

Other factors are truly external, and some act long rather than short term. All can have direct impact on markets and marketing opportunities, for good or ill. Consider a classic historic market change. In 1979, in the UK, the market for large motorbikes (those with engines over 250cc) was considerable and growing – with Japanese manufacturers predominating. Three years later the number sold had dropped to less than a quarter of the previous number. Why?

1. *Socially*: Fashions changed (it was the first yuppie period) and it became less socially acceptable to be a biker.
2. *Politically*: The law changed, making it more difficult and time-consuming to obtain a licence to ride a large bike.
3. *Technically*: The increasing technological sophistication of large bikes, particularly in their use of electronics, made home servicing and maintenance only possible for the most proficient and dedicated owners.
4. *Economically*: The inclusion of the more sophisticated elements inevitably necessitated raising buying prices (almost, in some cases, to the level of a small car).

It was the combined effect of all these factors which caused a major shift in the market. If such changes are not anticipated, or worse still, not recognised and acted on, then damage will be done; and, if competitors react more quickly or more effectively, then a company can be left behind. While we all have 20/20 hindsight (making it easy to look back to such cases), realistically such anticipation may not always be easy.

Watching the signs in areas such as these may well also create opportunities rather than restriction, as the following examples illustrate:

1. *Social*: Demographic trends (an ageing population in the UK and in other countries, such as Sweden and France) or lifestyle changes affect markets for many products. For example, older people may have more time to follow a hobby or enthusiasm that means they will buy more books on collecting, cosmology or computing, or go on holiday more often, etc.
2. *Political*: New government regulations can affect products very directly. For example, how many products and services – ranging from accounting services to seminars – are there currently linked to Britain and the European situation?
3. *Technical*: A technological development such as fax has created new product opportunities worldwide (and no doubt reduced the market for post and telex). Many businesses are now also increasingly affected by information technology, the 'information superhighway' and computers in all their rapidly-changing forms.
4. *Economic*: Reduced taxes affect price and thus demand. Major economic developments and, as a result, a better off (or more financially confident) population mean greater sales potential in all sorts of ways (more people able and willing to take holidays or make savings, investments, etc.). Increased taxes clearly have the opposite effect.

You can probably think of many more examples under these headings, including some close to home that you may be working on at present.

Marketing must always take place on a broad stage and marketing people must have broad vision to encompass all possible influences within the way they work.

**Definition:** *FMCG*

This is a classic piece of marketing jargon. The initials stand for: Fast Moving Consumer Goods, i.e. products such as packaged foods, toiletries and others typically sold through supermarkets and similar stores. The name is literal and the job of persuading someone to purchase a brand, say of tea, every week or so is different from that of persuading them to change their motor car every two or three years. The movement through the system is fast. The author once heard a conference speaker from a company who manufactured shotgun cartridges claim to be in 'the fastest kind of FMCG around'; it's a neat point, but not quite what the definition really means. (Other product group names are also used, for example 'white goods' which refer to consumer durables such as refrigerators and cookers.)

FMCG are different too from business-to-business or industrial marketing where one company sells to another.

**Definition:** *Impulse buy*

This term describes unplanned purchases. Most often these are minor items, such as the packet of mints you pick up near the checkout when you thought you had selected everything. Others can be more major, and some items are regularly bought this way, for example certain fashion products.

Marketing actively promotes the likelihood of impulse buys, for example by displaying products at the checkout to influence last-minute decisions before someone leaves the store. (See also DISPLAY AND MERCHANDISING.)

**Definition:** *International marketing*

See OVERSEAS MARKETING.

# Internal selling

**Introduction**

In a book directed largely to non-marketing people, it is worth making the point that selling is not solely an external activity. More generally, because selling is essentially only persuasive communication, it is, to a degree, true to say that everyone sells something. Much communication around a company is less than straightforward and, while not directed at customers, must still be made *persuasive*; making it so utilises exactly the techniques reviewed in the section SALES FORCE AND SELLING.

A case study is perhaps the best way to begin to explain internal selling. Consider the following situation.

Mr B runs the sales office for a medium-sized company. His team take customer enquiries, offer technical advice, handle queries of all kinds and take orders. Recent reorganisation has resulted in the merging of two departments. His people now occupy a large office together with the order-processing staff, who see to the invoicing and documentation. For the most part, all is going smoothly. However, the routing of telephone calls has become chaotic. The switchboard, despite having a note explaining who handles customers in which area of the country, is putting two out of three calls through to the wrong person, and the resulting confusion is upsetting staff and customers alike as calls have to be transferred.

Mr B carefully drafts and sends a memo to the personnel manager, to whom the switchboard operators report, complaining that the inefficiency of their service is upsetting customers and putting the company at risk of losing orders. He is surprised to find that far from the situation improving, all he gets is a defensive reply listing the total volume of calls with which the hard-pressed switchboard has to cope, citing other issues as of far more importance at present to the Personnel department and suggesting he takes steps to ensure customers ask for the right person.

Mr B intended to take prompt action that would improve customer service; he felt he had stated his case clearly and logically, yet all he succeeded in doing was rubbing a colleague up the wrong way. The problem remained. Think for a moment, before reading on, how else this might have been handled.

Here, the core of the communication was in writing. The memo Mr B sent, though well-intentioned, had the wrong effect, and would also have made any follow-up conversation (necessary because the problem had still to be resolved) more difficult.

From the way the case study is outlined above, we can imagine the sort of memo that was sent – probably something along the following lines:

---

**Memorandum**

To: Ms X, Personnel Manager
From: Mr B, Sales Office Manager
Subject: Customer Service

A recent analysis shows that, since the merging of the sales office and order-processing departments, two out of three incoming calls are misrouted by the switchboard and have to be transferred.

This wastes time and, more important, is seen by customers as inefficient. As the whole intention of this department is to ensure prompt, efficient service to our customers, this is not only a frustration internally, it also risks damaging the image customers have of the organisation and, at worst, losing orders.

I would be grateful if you could have a word with the supervisor and operators on the switchboard to ensure that the situation is rectified before serious damage results.

---

The problem is certainly identified, the implications of it continuing are spelt out, and a solution – briefing of the relevant staff by the personnel manager – is suggested. The intention, as has been said, is good. However, despite a degree of politeness – 'I would be grateful . . .' – it is easy to read the overall tone of the message as a criticism. Furthermore, the solution is vague: tell them what exactly? It seems to be leaving a great deal to Personnel. Maybe Mr B felt, 'it is not my fault, they should sort it out'. To an extent this may be true, but you often have to choose between a line which draws attention to a problem and one which sets out to get something done. They are often two different things.

In this case the key objective is to change the action, and to do so quickly before customer relations are damaged. This is more important than having a dig at Personnel, and worth taking a moment over. Although a matter of overall company concern, it is primarily of more immediate concern to the sales office.

So what should Mr B have done? To ensure attention, collaboration and action, his memo needed to:

- make the problem clear
- avoid undue criticism, or turning the matter into an emotive issue
- spell out a solution
- make that solution easy and acceptable to those in Personnel (including the switchboard operators themselves).

Perhaps with that in mind, his memo should have been more like the following:

---

**Memorandum**

To: Ms X, Personnel Manager
From: Mr B, Sales Office Manager
Subject: Customer Service

The recent merger of the sales office and order-processing departments seems to have made some problems for the switchboard.

You will find that I have set out in this note something about what is happening and why, and specific suggestions to put it right. You will see the suggested action is mainly with myself, but I would like to be sure that you approve before proceeding.

**The problem**

Two out of every three calls coming in are misrouted and have to be transferred. This wastes time both in my department and on the switchboard and is likely to be seen as inefficient by customers. To preserve customer relations, and perhaps ultimately orders, it needs to be sorted out promptly.

**The reason**

Apart from the sheer volume of calls, always a problem at this time of the year, the problem is one of information. The switchboard operators have insufficient information to help guide them, and what they do has been outdated by the departmental merger. Given clear guidance, neither they, nor customers, will have any problems.

**Action**

What I would suggest, therefore, is the following action:

1 I have prepared a note (and map) showing which member of staff

---

deals with customers from which geographical area, and would like to make this available for reference on the switchboard.

2   This might be best introduced at a short briefing and, if we could assemble the operators for ten minutes before the board opens one morning, I could do that with them and answer any questions.

3   Longer term, it would be useful if the operators visited our department and saw something of what goes on. We could arrange a rota and do this over a few lunch hours so that it can be fitted in conveniently.

If this seems a practical approach do let me know and I will put matters in hand.

This is not set out as the 'right' or guaranteed approach, but it is certainly better than before. It is more likely to work because it follows the rules set out above. In particular, it:

- lays no blame
- recognises that Personnel and the switchboard are important
- considers their needs – for clear guidance, for being able to handle the volume more easily, for someone else to take the action
- anticipates objections, e.g. who will do all this
- is specific in terms of action – who will do what.

There seems every chance it will have the desired effect. Many situations exhibit similar characteristics. All it needs is a clear, systematic approach that recognises the other person's point of view, and *sells* the desired action.

Next time you are faced with something similar, try this sort of approach; you might be surprised at how well it works, and how persuasive you can be.

# Internet marketing

**Introduction**

The internet is currently changing as one watches, clearly showing how marketing is dynamic and must constantly react to, take advantage of or beware of, new elements.

The internet is in its early stages, and the record of accurate prediction in the area of developing technology is not good (whatever happened to the paperless office we were promised fifteen years ago?). Essentially, the internet offers new options in terms of distribution (and for the customer purchase method); see DISTRIBUTION.

Already the internet is providing new facilities: it is an alternative to catalogues, where customers can look up and check out what they might buy. But it goes further. It can be interactive. For example, it is possible to check out a hotel not only by looking at pictures or finding out prices, but also by 'walking through' it in virtual reality. The internet also offers direct sale and ordering facilities: once 'logged on' using a computer, a modem and then a credit card, you can place an order and goods can be dispatched to you with no further contact; you can order a pizza or buy a car.

For some companies this represents an opportunity; but there are dangers. Not everyone is on the internet, indeed many (the older generation?) will never be, and directing too much marketing effort towards it may alienate certain groups of potential customers. It will be a long time before it is the way to market products to individual customers in rural India, but there are clearly opportunities, and experience is greater in some countries than in the UK.

It will be interesting to see how it develops; both customers and companies will doubtless watch closely to see how it can help them in future.

**Warning**

The first comments of this section are all too true. Prediction of developments as radical and fast-changing as this are fraught with difficulty. Jumping unthinkingly towards something may provide a breakthrough; or it may court disaster. Caution as well as the willingness to stick necks out is called for, and testing is a wise precaution.

# Key accounts

## Introduction

Large accounts, for that is what key accounts tend to be, need special handling. They also represent special opportunities for sales and profit.

Let us start with the fact that key accounts are often powerful. For example, as with certain other businesses, a large proportion of total publishing business goes through a small number of large distributors – the large retail chains such as W. H. Smith, Menzies, Dillons, etc. To exploit the market to any real extent, any publisher *has* to trade with them. Similar situations also exist in other markets – food products and major supermarket groups are another well known example; and sometimes the distributor will exploit the power this gives them to:

- squeeze for preferential – and ever larger – discounts; these will sometimes be used to facilitate the cutting of the price of the product
- force suppliers to produce similar products to their own for the distributor, who then sells these 'own brands' at a lower price – these brands are a major feature of many consumer goods markets
- limit the supplier's role to that of producing goods to the distributor's specification at the lowest possible mark-up; in some businesses certain trends may be most influenced from the retailer end.

*Note: This is an example of what is called Pareto's Law (so called after an Italian mathematician of that name) or the '80/20 rule'. This refers to the common occurrence of, in this case, 80 per cent of sales and/or profit coming from 20 per cent of customers (similarly products where there is a range). The numbers will not be exact, but this kind of ratio occurs in a number of marketing areas (others include product range and mix) and should, when it does, prompt organisational action.*

Many companies manage their dealings with major customers on a different basis from more normal-sized ones and have staff with titles such as 'Major Account Executive' to do so; this is sensible as major customers are not just different in scale, but in nature, demanding different skills, such as negotiation, and processes to handle them effectively.

The sales job here is characterised by the desire of the supplier to create an effective ongoing business relationship; and to characterise that as something the customer wants. In a competitive environment the pressure here is considerable. Not all relationships are equally well regarded by customers and some suppliers do better than others.

---

**Definition:** *Loyalty schemes*

This term describes marketing activity aimed at initiating and maintaining purchasing habits, holding customers with an organisation and discouraging movement to competition. Such schemes as those offering incentives to frequent fliers, or those card schemes now operated by certain supermarket chains are examples of this technique.

See also SALES PROMOTION.

---

**Definition:** *Mail order marketing*

Nothing very complicated here, the term simply means goods supplied through the post. This might be from an advertisement, or from a catalogue. It is worth noting that an enormous range of goods is now sold by mail order; as well as the large catalogue companies such as Gratton, there is a plethora of smaller and specialist operators selling everything from books (e.g. The Book People), to fashion (e.g. Racing Green), to office stationery and furniture (e.g. Neat Ideas).

Some well-known catalogues operate from a retail base (e.g. Habitat) utilising two means of distribution to maximise sales. The detailed promotional techniques of this form of marketing are rather specialised; some light may be cast on this by the section DIRECT MAIL as when goods go by post, often the promotion does too.

# Market mapping

Using a market map can quickly show the complexities and links and chains involved. Figure 5 shows on a flowchart basis the way in which books (like this one, perhaps) are marketed. Even this is simplified: there are several

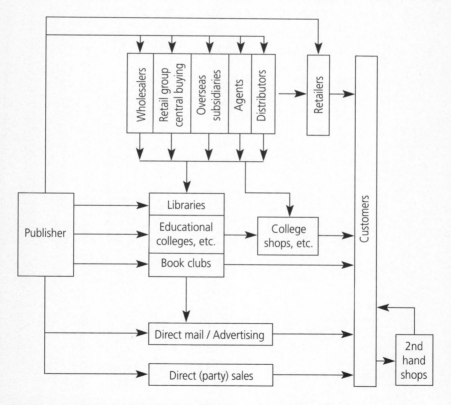

*Figure 5  Market map showing distributive chains in publishing*

kinds of wholesaler; the educational category could well be expanded to include professional bodies – general ones such as The Institute of Management, or specific ones such as The Institute of Chartered Accountants, both of which sell books, the latter on a narrower front than the former; retailers can include everything from a major book shop to quite different kinds of shops which sell some books, such as supermarkets or tourist offices selling guide books – the range of outlets selling books has expanded over the years and no doubt still has further to go.

Given all this complexity and the many options, deciding on, organising and managing the chosen option (or options) is an important task. Clearly, as Figure 5 shows, distribution can entail a number of levels – or steps, as they are sometimes called – and therefore involve large numbers of external organisations and people.

Such complexities, and the fact that the marketing job to be done differs down different 'routes' (because the nature and needs of those that must be related to differs) make this sort of analysis very useful. It can help decide priorities, show up gaps and flag additional opportunities, and generally help keep marketing's attitude to the distributive process on the ball.

# *Market research*

To help define the terms involved, and make clear the purpose of research in this context, the following is quoted from the book *The Effective Use of Market Research* (Kogan Page, 1992) by Robin Birn, with whom I have worked regularly over some years and who runs Strategy, Research and Action Ltd. It is an excellent reference book for anyone who wants to know more about market research.

> Decision-making is central to carrying out managerial functions to make the planning and monitoring process work. Good decisions are taken on the basis of availability and use of relevant information. The information of most concern to marketing management comes from markets and customers, present, potential and future, and concerns the shape, size, nature, needs, opportunities and threats within the market. Market research is the means of providing them with that information.

## Definition of market research

The traditional definition of market research is: *'The systematic problem analysis, model-building and fact-finding for the purpose of improved decision-making and control in the marketing of goods and services.'*

This implies that research is not just an information tool but a means of providing guidance to help improve the abilities of management within an organisation, as well as a means of making a contribution to the management of the marketing mix. It can be used to help decide on: the marketing strategy required to meet the challenge of new opportunities; which market gaps to approach; and which are the key areas of interest for future marketing strategies.

## Purposes of market research

The two basic purposes of research are:

- to reduce uncertainty when plans are being made, whether these relate to the marketing operation as a whole or to individual components of the marketing mix such as advertising or sales promotion
- to monitor performance after the plans have been put into operation; the monitoring role has two specific functions – it helps to control the execution of the company's operational plan and it makes a substantial contribution to long-term strategic planning.

Simply stated, research covers all the 'finding out' activities of marketing. It is the essential first stage of a marketing function – the identification of consumer needs. It describes five major types of research:

1. *Market research*: Who buys what in what quantity?
2. *Product research*: What is right and wrong with the products of the company, or part of them?
3. *Marketing method research*: Are we communicating and distributing effectively?
4. *Motivational research*: Why do people buy the products they do and what do they feel about them?
5. *Attitude surveys*: What are customers' attitudes to the products and to the companies which make them?

Like any other form of research, marketing research can only investigate past behaviour. This is of course very helpful in predicting future behaviour but research as such cannot be conducted on the future. When attempts are made (opinion polling, intention surveys, etc.) then serious errors can be made.

The role of research, therefore, is to improve the fact basis on which forecasts and decisions are made. The difference between researching the past and predicting the future must be clearly recognised.

## The role of market research

It is worth spelling out in a little more detail the range involved here. Market research provides information which assists an organisation to define opportunities for product development and market strategy. It works by assessing whether marketing strategies are well targeted, and identifying market opportunities or changes that are required by customers. Market research tends to confirm issues that are well known in a market initially, but if planned well and effectively it will also identify new opportunities, market niches or ways by which to improve sales, marketing and communications activities.

The role of market research, therefore, is to reduce uncertainty in decision-making, monitor the effects of decisions taken and identify the performance of a company or a product in the market.

To be more specific, we can list five key uses for market research:

- to identify the size, shape and nature of a market, so as to understand the market and marketing opportunities
- to investigate the strengths and weaknesses of competitive products and the level of trade support a company enjoys
- to test out strategic and product ideas which help to define the most effective customer led strategies
- to monitor the effectiveness of strategies
- to help to define when marketing expenditure, promotions and targeting need to be adjusted or improved.

The variety of purpose here makes it clear that market research is not simply a 'first check': it *is* useful ahead of any action, but it also provides a means of checking and refining as operations proceed. Companies, especially those for whom budgets always seem tight, who have selected one of these uses for market research are concerned to make the research a worthwhile investment. Best results come when their marketing and sales planning is influenced by the results.

To illustrate further, some of the regular and main reasons for using market research are as follows:

- to provide data on the market, or a market segment, and to discover whether the sector is increasing, staying the same or decreasing in importance to customers
- to obtain information to help to understand who the customers are, and the way in which they buy and use certain products
- to evaluate customer service, assessing what customers feel about the services they are receiving
- to research customer attitudes and needs on a continuous basis to know which product types are selling and where there are opportunities for new sales
- to achieve better targeting, understanding what media and messages influence consumers to buy the products

- to identify changes in the market which will affect how marketing must proceed in future.

## Sources of information

This too is an important area. Sources include:

1. *Internal records*: A prime source which, when processed, can reveal much about the characteristics of customers, what they buy and how.
2. *Published information*: This can be from various sources.
3. *Field surveys*: These should only be used when the first two sources are exhausted or they will simply discover (very expensively) what is already known.

## Research techniques

1. *Sampling*: In most markets, to contain the research within practical limits, sampling must be used. This uses probability theory to predict the characteristics of a total universe from a small section within definable limits. The commonest sampling methods are random and quota, particularly the latter as it is cheaper to implement.
2. *The questionnaire*: This must be carefully designed to ensure the forming of the questions does not bias the answer.
3. *Research methods*: Questionnaires can be administered in person, on the telephone, or by post. There is an inverse correlation between accuracy and cost. In certain types of research, e.g. motivational studies, group interviews are often used.

## Running a research project

Management must first decide as precisely as possible what it wishes to know. To ask for 'everything about the market' is very expensive and often unusable.

Secondly, it must decide whether to use internal staff (either researchers or other personnel, e.g. the sales force) or an outside agency. When the costs and possible prejudices of internal staff are considered, it is often at least equally economic to use specialists.

The project brief and method must be clearly defined and acceptable tolerances and timings set. If outsiders are being used, several proposals should be sought to ensure the fullest possible exploration of the problem. When the findings are available, they should be checked against any other data and an action programme of decisions drawn up, based on the facts identified. Otherwise, although very interesting, the survey will become yet another item clogging the filing system.

## The value of research

For research to give the value it should, management must define:

- What decisions do we have to make?
- When?
- On what information will they be based?
- How accurate does the information need to be?
- How quickly do we need it?

No company can risk operating without research, even though the 'research' is purely deep experience of company staff. As decisions get bigger, however, it is worth the insurance of real research to establish a better fact basis.

To conclude, I will again quote Robin Birn. In *The Effective Use of Market Research* he describes the results of using research as a 'win-win' situation, and defines it so neatly it seems unfair to paraphrase the thought. The two examples that follow, taken from the same source, emphasise the practical contribution research can make to marketing and to marketing planning.

> Using research is a 'win-win' situation for those who interpret it and action it effectively. Management wins first time when the research confirms its prejudices, ideas and experiences so providing reassurances that it is taking the right decisions. It wins a second time if the research provides new information or gives a new focus or emphasis on the subject being researched.
>
> Over a period of time users of research also find that they win a third time. If they take a step back to look at the original findings of the research objectively then they can design more interesting and more relevant research than had been completed originally. Research therefore helps management to win by indicating the action it needs to take.

## Reappraising the results: two examples

The first example involves a packaging company whose main product base was the manufacture of high-quality printed cartons and boxes. The company had recently invested in the most modern production plant, capable of producing superior quality products at lower costs and with a reduced turn-around compared to their competitors. Once the plant was in operation, it was realised that the necessary production volumes were not being achieved from the sales orders to make the plant viable. So the company decided to carry out market research with its existing and potential customers, to establish its market profile before deciding how to develop a strategy to obtain an increase in market share.

In-depth interviews were carried out with the major purchasers in the market to establish their attitudes towards the leading suppliers of packaging in terms of price, delivery, quality and general company image. Each individual supplier was rated in these terms against the other suppliers. The original packaging company had believed that the results would show the company to be among the leaders in quality and delivery performance, but average in terms of price.

The market research results, however, were not as expected. In fact, the results suggested that the company was bottom of the league on all factors except quality. In addition, it showed that the company had an overall image of being a 'slow reacting company', only to be used for special work not required quickly and where price was not important.

These results obviously surprised the company and did not provide the answer to how to increase the volume throughput and the commercial viability of the production plant. As the results were being considered by management, certain more positive features became apparent.

First, they realised that the quality image was favourable and that it was a major reason why the company had the image of being a specialist work supplier. Secondly, the comments on poor delivery had been those associated with the company before its investment programme, and the buyers interviewed were not necessarily aware of the new plant and production facilities. Lastly, the perception of specialist work did not link with pricing, which was considered unimportant in this area.

Clearly, the company's initial marketing strategy of being a high-volume, low-cost and quality producer was at variance with the market's image. It was also apparent from the results that a more significant market niche was available. Since its image was specialist, and once the message of increased volume with rapid delivery could be passed into the market, it would be possible for the company to increase its market share. More importantly, as this type of work was not price-sensitive, higher profits could be made without direct comparison to competitive suppliers.

Here we have seen that the expected results of the market research were not obtained and the company's initial marketing approach appeared to be failing. As a result of the market research, intuitive analysis of the outcome showed that a definite marketing approach was possible which could provide greater success than had initially been targeted in the marketing plan. The market research gave the company much more actionable results than had been thought possible in the initial marketing planning.

## Research on 'autopilot'

A brief word about a second, rather different, example makes an additional point. The company involved manufactured pharmaceutical products.

Any pharmaceutical product is necessarily subject to many tests before it can be marketed to the public (a complex process which in most countries is regulated by government). The last stage consists of clinical trials; i.e. doctors use the product with a limited number of patients and report back to the producer.

The company was launching a new product, a gel to treat mouth ulcers, and had reached the stage of clinical trials. Information was slow to come in and the marketing manager became concerned about the effect on the subsequent schedules and launch date. His secretary, aware of this, thought about it and had an idea. It seemed so obvious that, for a while, not wishing to appear foolish in suggesting something which had been thought of and rejected for good reason, she said nothing. But, as the delay became worse she plucked up courage. 'Surely', she said, 'the people who would hear about patients with mouth ulcers are not doctors, they're dentists.' Eureka! They had not thought of it (all previous products had clearly been for prescription by doctors); the test was restarted with a panel of dentists and, in due course, the launch proceeded on time.

The moral here is that many aspects of the marketing process need ideas, and most marketing people do not mind who has them, as long as they have sufficient to keep the process working effectively. In the kind of circumstances described above, the worst that could have happened would have been that the idea was seen as inappropriate; while it could not then have been used, the interest taken would no doubt have been applauded. The situation is always wide open; the next idea might be one that matters.

Note: *The term marketing research, as opposed to market research, is used to specify the area that such research investigates. It is research into marketing methods (such as the effectiveness of advertising) rather than markets and the likes, dislikes and behaviour of customers (which is called market research). With the usual precision that the marketing world brings to its jargon, marketing research may also be used less precisely as an umbrella term for all research in the marketing area: that is marketing and market research.*

**Warning**

For all its strengths it must never be forgotten that research can only ever provide part of the answer, particularly when decisions affecting future action are required. Judgement (and experience) must always go hand in hand with research.

# Market segments

**Introduction**

There is seldom a mass market for any product, though some companies presume that mass-marketing and advertising methods will successfully exploit such a mass market. Analysis has shown, however, that within each overall market there is actually a number of what are called 'market segments'. This is true not only for common products which would be expected to have a mass market, such as breakfast cereals, soap and basic clothing, but also for other products, such as industrial components and equipment, and for services, such as hotels or accountants.

Within a market, each segment represents a group of actual and potential customers with the same needs which can be satisfied by similar products. Compare this with some other everyday situations: for example, within one overall market for cars there are segments interested particularly in economy, status, carrying capacity, etc.; and with detergents there are segments interested in softness (for either the hands or clothes), cleaning power, persistent stain removal, economy, etc. In industrial markets the same applies. Instead of mass-marketing, therefore, such segments often have to be tackled selectively and individually in order to achieve maximum profitability and the least conflict over the image of the company and its product.

Segments are not something a company invents; they have to be researched and discovered, accurately identified, characterised and then exploited individually. The key characteristics of a segment, inherently showing how it lends itself to exploitation, are as follows:

* homogeneous
* all consumers in it share the same needs profile
* desirable
* sufficiently large to offer adequate opportunity for the fulfilment of corporate product objectives
* accessible
* can be reached cost- or time-effectively
* measurable

- its potential can be quantified and qualified.

Just to clarify a little more jargon as we go, it should be noted that 'niche' marketing refers to the smallest and most precisely identified end of market segments, where marketing can 'fine-tune' its focus, directing activity more and more accurately towards groups most likely to respond. It thus usually describes a highly prescribed approach to marketing which specifically exploits such a group and builds business from it.

---

**Definition:** *Marketing*

Marketing can be a confusing term. The word is used in a number of different ways: the marketing function; concept; process, etc.

The *Introduction* is designed to put all this in perspective. See page xi.

# *Marketing control*

## Introduction

Management control is essential in any part of the business, and marketing is no exception. We will not go into great detail here, but a number of matters are, however, worth brief comment.

## Organising the marketing function

In order to achieve its objectives, some form of planning system is needed. This, in turn, demands an organisation structure both to create marketing plans (see MARKETING PLANNING) and to implement them. Being a *marketing* organisation (i.e. consumer-needs orientated), the structure should be built from the bottom up. This process starts by identifying what services consumers desire from the company in order to be persuaded to buy. This will help specify the nature and scale of, for example, the sales effort required.

Likewise, the management structure of this field operation can be identified by asking what support the subordinates need in terms of nature and scale in order that their activities are effective and controlled. Whatever the form of marketing organisation adopted, care must be given to its integration with other functions of the company.

Control in marketing is conceptually similar to other forms of management control. It depends upon the comparison of actual performance (A) against pre-set standards (S) and the taking of corrective action based upon the resulting variances (V): $A - S = +/- V$.

The objectives and plans will form the basis of the standards. Thus, for example, the sales plan will contain sales forecasts which can be translated into targets for each salesperson. Many of the promotion areas have been traditionally viewed as immeasurable. Undoubtedly it is difficult to assess and control activities which, for the large part, depend upon human reaction and which cannot be easily separated from other influences. The difficulty has been exacerbated, however, by attempting to evaluate each part in terms of the whole. Thus, 'How much will advertising affect sales?' is usually an unanswerable question as sales do not depend upon advertising alone.

If, however, it is clearly specified what the advertising is supposed to do, i.e. impress a certain message on a certain number of people of a certain type, then it is feasible to define standards of performance and evaluate achievement.

Certainly, control of a different kind can and should be exercised in marketing. All marketing activities are quantifiable in money terms and thus budgetary control can be exercised.

For marketing activities to be effective it is not enough that each department should be well run. The whole marketing function needs to be integrated and well co-ordinated with the rest of the company.

## Implementing and controlling the plan

A marketing plan, deriving from a SWOT analysis and the other processes referred to in discussing marketing planning (see SWOTs), should spell out three key elements of the activity that it plans. These are:

- objectives (specifying the corporate *destination*)
- strategies (the *road* taken to reach that destination)
- tactics (the *vehicle* used to travel along the strategic road).

Beyond that, successful implementation depends upon the effective management of five resources:

1. *What*: The goals, objectives, aims
2. *Who*: The people responsible/accountable for plan realisation
3. *Where*: The specific, identified, quantified market places
4. *When*: The period covered by the plan
5. *Why*: The reasons, desired outcomes.

It will be perhaps a marketing manager's responsibility to ensure that all material marketing resources are in place. These could well comprise:

- product
- packaging
- internal promotion aids (sales aids)
- external promotion campaigns (e.g. advertising)
- budgetary management systems
- sales data systems
- performance standards.

Once the plan is launched, the emphasis of attention changes to *control*. The plan should contain specific financial, marketing, sales, distribution and promotion objectives. These provide a basis for performance standards in a number of key areas, including product sales (in value terms), product sales (in volume terms) and product sales (in market share terms).

Performance standards can be expressed as follows:

1. *Annual targets*: These express performance expectations in sales, profit and market share terms. Annual targets are known as *absolute targets*. Variances to these targets will identify what has gone right or wrong, but not why.
2. *Moving standards*: These express the annual targets in moving divisions of the plan period, i.e. monthly or quarterly actuals, cumulatives and trends. Again, although moving standards can forecast deviations from plan, they will not identify why performance is greater or less than the required targets.
3. *Diagnostic standards*: These *can* identify what is causing the variations and why, and may indicate an appropriate action.

## Variance analysis

Variances are calculated by comparing actual results against the pre-set standards or targets. First, cumulative totals can be used so that individual monthly variations will tend to cancel each other out. Secondly, moving annual totals (MATs) can be used by taking twelve months' performance up to and including the month in question. As each month is added and the same month of the previous year is deducted, the trend in *moving annual total* will indicate present performance compared with the same period in the previous year.

This procedure enables comparisons to be made on a single diagram of monthly performance against target, cumulative performance against target and, via the moving annual total, the present year versus the previous year (see also Z CHART).

The benefit of a good control system and feedback mechanism is that it enables a manager quickly to *identify sales performance variances and the true reason for them*, and to *react to changed circumstances*. Controlling the plan makes it possible to report monthly, and answer the following questions which may be raised by top management:

• Are the plan objectives being met?
• What are the variances between budget and actual?
• What are the causes of these variances?
• What actions are being taken to correct them?
• Is a re-forecast/re-budget necessary?

Marketing will not guarantee success but, carefully applied and well monitored, it will certainly increase the likelihood of success. It is important to make sure that success is in precisely the terms specified by the organisation, i.e. with reference to the overall financial ratios (such as Return on Capital Employed) that have been agreed.

Simply, control answers the final question, and also allows opportunity for fine-tuning of performance, a hand on the tiller to adjust course when things are not going exactly to plan and, just as important, the possibility to take advantage of changes which present, sometimes unexpected, new opportunities. With this in mind, we see how important co-ordination is to the marketing process. The progression from planning to implementation to control in a continuing cycle (see Figure 6) is as important overall as any of the individual elements; together they make the process work. With all of this, good factual information is the basis of the best decisions, and any source of good information is to be welcomed.

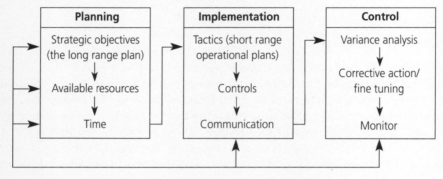

*Figure 6  Implementing and controlling the marketing plan*

---

**Definition:**  *Marketing culture*

Because marketing is broad in its scope and must, by definition, involve many people throughout the organisation in various ways, its success is directly affected by the way those people interface with and support marketing.

If people around the organisation understand this interdependence and play their part well, then there is said to be a good marketing culture. The term also implies that marketing people have a very good focus on the market and on customers.

A good marketing culture is something an organisation needs to work actively at creating. Some of what is said in the *Introduction* is relevant here; see also MISSION STATEMENTS.

# Marketing mix

**Introduction**

This term describes 'the offering' of the company to the market, and consists of three elements:

1. *Product* range
2. *Prices*, including discounts and terms policy
3. *Presentation*, or means of communicating with the market (selling, sales promotion, advertising, etc.).

Note: *Sometimes four 'P's are listed as the marketing mix, the fourth being 'place'. Certainly, the place where business is done (home markets and/or overseas, for example) is important; this is touched on elsewhere. Juggling with these three elements enables a company to balance its internal objectives with those of its customers.*

There is clearly a complex and inherent relationship between the elements of the mix mentioned above. For example, a company may want to charge higher prices, but only be able to make this possible with a product change that improves value.

The effect of technological development and the vigorous competition that exists in a capitalist society has resulted in products and prices of competing companies in many industries becoming increasingly similar. This 'commodity' problem is obvious with something like motor cars, so many appear almost identical, or hotels – 'if it's Monday it must be Holiday Inn'.

Because of this commodity factor, the first two elements of the marketing mix – product and price – are becoming less important to customer choice, and presentation (the way in which the company tells the market about products and prices) has become crucial. Often it is the only differentiating element between companies. Perhaps some products and brands are themselves so strong that they surmount this factor, but usually this is a situation that has painstakingly been achieved over some time, and is supported by promotion to make the impact last.

Presentation includes the whole gamut of communication techniques, including advertising, promotion (including everything from schemes like consumer competitions to catalogues and point-of-sale material), direct mail, personal selling, merchandising (controlled for many suppliers largely by the retailers they sell through), packaging (which includes physical packaging – getting products to stockists and/or customers in good condition – though packaging is an advertisement too) and aspects of service (now often referred to as customer care).

All these have not only to play their part in persuasion, but also to create a positive image, and a difference in perception, both by emphasising real product differences and/or adding something extra. The extra element may well be intangible, but this does not make it any less real. For instance, all watches tell the time, and these days usually do so accurately. But some sell primarily on fashion considerations (Swatch) or status (Rolex). The fact that there is rarely one simple factor but a multitude of interlinking ones makes for greater complexity. Watches, to continue the example, are bought for many reasons – often as presents – and selecting a particular model may involve consideration of price, design, status, fashion, brand image, features (does it tell you the date, or the phases of the moon?) and many other factors.

The ranking of these factors will differ to a degree for different people; and many decisions about product purchase will have a similar complexity of decision. Overall, perhaps the most important factor, however it may be stated, is value for money.

All this may make it sound as if marketing people can elect to exert influence as and where they want. Not so; there are other restraints (see EXTERNAL FACTORS).

# *Marketing planning*

**Introduction**

It is axiomatic that one of the things marketing should do is to act in a way that is directional to the business, driving it towards whatever commercial objectives are chosen. In this section we focus on planning, showing that it sets the scene for how products and services are promoted.

## Why plan?

Plans are important. Every management guru has their own version of a maxim to the effect that 'if you don't know where you're going, any path will do' – a sentiment that was put with much more style and elegance by Lewis Carroll in *Alice in Wonderland*:

> 'Would you tell me, please, which way I ought to walk from here?'
> 'That depends a good deal on where you want to get to', said the Cat.
> 'I don't much care where . . .' said Alice.
> 'Then it doesn't matter which way you walk', said the Cat.
> 'So long as I get *somewhere*', Alice added, as an explanation.
> 'Oh, you're sure to do that', said the Cat, 'if you only walk long enough.'

However it is said, it is good advice. Every organisation needs clear objectives. And these must be helpful in a practical sense. If they are too simple, and if the planning that goes with them is too academic, or simply too voluminous, then they are not likely to influence the business, still less to do so positively.

Plans should have a degree of formality and should be in writing, even in the smallest company (but a document like a telephone directory that takes forever to prepare and then just gathers dust on a shelf is not to be recommended). Plans must, if they are to be useful, set out not only *what* will be done, but *how* it will be achieved (and should also address the question of who will be involved in the action and when). These intentions must be met so that:

- it is certain that all the objectives set by a firm are clearly related to specific actions (and that other actions, less focused on key activities, do not distract from achieving objectives)

- priorities are flagged and staff throughout the organisation know what these are, so that action at every level is directed accurately towards agreed objectives
- all activities specified in the plan can be linked to measurement, assessment and control to enable fine tuning as the year and the plan progress.

Exactly how an individual company puts together its plan depends on its size, style and other factors. The intention here is not to set down a fixed planning process, but to review some of the aspects of marketing that are directly related to planning.

The key purpose of all such longer-term planning is to make the ultimate day-to-day running of the business easier and more certain; more likely to produce the desired results. For many organisations a key aspect of the thinking that goes into planning and choice of direction and action is research (see MARKET RESEARCH); this assembles a basis of hard information from which decisions can be taken and risk kept as low as possible.

A systematic approach to the planning process is essential if it is to be practical and useful; this is commented on below.

## Compiling the marketing plan

As was said at the start of this section, a plan is – or should be – of real value in creating action that will generate business success. Goals must be set and, perhaps above all, action plans must be in place to ensure that the right things are done at the right time. Compiling the marketing plan is a task that may involve a number of people, from the managing director down, around the sales and marketing side of the company and across to involve other functions such as finance. But it must be co-ordinated by whoever has overall marketing responsibility, and contributed to by others. You may like to consider who is, or should be, involved in your company.

Without getting immersed in too much detail, and leaving the question of the variety of strategic options on one side (see MARKETING STRATEGIES) the main stages involved are as follows:

### 1. *Formulate overall direction and goal*

This stage must answer the question: 'What business are we in?' If the business is looked at in terms of customers, not the product, then the right orientation to the company can be developed. Needs and benefits, not functions or features, should be the focus. As the president of Revlon once famously said: 'In the factory we make cosmetics, but in the drug-store we sell hope'. In any organisation this kind of clarity is equally valuable and acts to focus effort. Presumably companies such as Dixons or The Body Shop, to pick by way of example two retailers that are distinctive in quite different ways, have a clear view of the area of business they wish to concentrate on (at least for the moment).

It is too easy to become myopic and see only what the company currently sells; the danger is that as market needs change they are not recognised, not recognised fully or accurately, or perception of them lags behind reality. Business definitions should be narrow enough to provide direction, yet broad enough to allow the growth and response to changing market needs that are necessary. The most productive approach is to define a business in terms of the needs it can satisfy and the segments of the market it can service. Thus, in order to be able to satisfy a market need and by so doing make a profit, a company needs to look critically at itself. The classic approach to this is the 'SWOTs' (or SWOT) analysis. SWOTs stands for: strengths, weaknesses/opportunities, threats. The final 's' simply acknowledges that these are plural. There is nothing daunting about it; it is simply a convenient, systematic way of reviewing the situation within (SW) and outside (OT) the company. It suggests not so much a massive one-off analysis, rather an ongoing 'rolling' review, which an annual plan may simply update and formalise.

The first task is thus to look internally at the organisation and identify:

- its strengths – what it is *good* at doing
- its weaknesses – what it is *bad* at doing.

Subsequent plans can then concentrate on:

- exploiting, perpetuating or extending strengths
- avoiding, minimising or eradicating weaknesses
- converting weaknesses into strengths, e.g. by training.

(See also SWOTs.)

## 2. *Identify the external opportunities*

The aim here is to determine the market potential in terms of needs that are not being fully satisfied. The needs of all segments should be considered. This stage of the process involves segmentation of the total market, and often indicates where market research should be directed. This overall area links to the considerable detail of planning exactly which products or services will be marketed. Each individual decision is important, each must take a market view and overall success or failure is linked to each of these decisions and their cumulative effect (we look again at exactly how such decisions are made a little later). Such decisions must also accommodate the thinking involved in stage 2.

### 3. *Identify the external threats*

As well as identifying opportunities and threats from customers, it is important to consider the threat to existing revenue and profit. This will come from competition, demand and the many other environmental factors which surround marketing.

This stage of the process involves collecting data, the making of assumptions and the production of forecasts for the business.

### 4. *Analyse internal strengths and weaknesses to produce marketing objectives and strategies*

The marketing planning process is concerned with how the resources available to the company can be used to exploit the opportunity.

Marketing goals must be realistic – this is achieved by analysing strengths and weaknesses and asking: 'Why should we be able to exploit the market opportunities we have identified?' (and How? since such planning is ultimately action planning or it is of little use).

Generating strategies is essentially a creative task. Ideally, the more alternatives that are generated the better. A good strategy will identify the main lines of business activity which will remain constant over the total planning period and provide the framework for tactical decision-making. Strategy aims to answer the question: 'What basic activities should we carry out?' Marketing strategies are explored further in another section (see MARKETING STRATEGIES).

### 5. *Programme the marketing mix*

Within the framework defined by the strategy, this stage is concerned with determining the detailed programmes and action plans that will allow attainment of the goals. The overall approach involves:

- breaking down the marketing mix into: the product elements, the pricing elements, the promotion elements
- programming the activities of each
- integrating the separate programmes of each into the marketing plan.

### 6. *Communication and control*

The various elements of promotion are concerned with identifying and implementing the most appropriate *communication* activity between the company and its potential customers. It integrates the activities of personal selling with those of non-personal selling: advertising, public relations (PR), sales promotion and merchandising, and concerns decisions on the methods and types of sales effort required. This area must accommodate what the company can do independently and what it needs to work on with the approval or collaboration of others. For example, it is no good planning a consumer product launch around elaborate retail window displays if agreement from retailers is unlikely to be forthcoming, or if launch and promotion do not match in timing terms.

Once the plan has been approved it can be communicated; this is important and the plan should act as a major influence to ensure that everyone in the company knows – and shares – a common view and sees how their own activities fit in with the whole. This means that the plan should be practical, well written and succinct. The final format of the plan must be such as to encourage revisions before senior management confirms its adoption.

*Controls* consist of bringing actual and desired results closer together. It is a four-stage process:

- setting standards
- collecting information
- variance analysis
- corrective action.

Clearly, as has been mentioned above, more people than simply the marketing manager and immediate staff will be involved in the creation of a marketing plan.

> *Note:* It is stages 2 to 4 here that primarily make up the SWOTs process touched on earlier. Such considerations are, of course, specific to any individual organisation. The section on SWOTs gives an example, summarising the sort of questions that need asking and which perhaps indicate that much more detail needs to be considered.

The old saying 'plan the work and work the plan' is good advice. Marketing planning is not an academic exercise, nor should it create a strait-jacket which stifles flexibility or, still worse, creativity. It is more akin to a route map; it sets out the broad intention, and does so in sufficient detail to prompt the action appropriate to achieving objectives. But it also helps along the way. It makes possible any necessary fine-tuning, not only to take corrective action if targets are not being met, but also to take advantage of additional opportunities met during the year. This is important in a dynamic market where rapid response to what, say, customers or competitors do may be vital.

In many ways the basis for marketing planning springs essentially from asking, and answering, three key questions:

1. Where are we now?
2. Where do we want to go?
3. How will we get there?

and sets the scene for a fourth – How will we know when we get there? – to be answered. This latter links to the aspect of control.

Finally, let us summarise the elements that should be, manageably, documented in any such plan. These include:

- a statement of assumptions made about economic, technological, social and political developments (both short and long term)
- a review of the sales/profit results of the company (by product – or product category – market and geographical break-down) in the previous period
- an analysis of external opportunities and threats
- an analysis of internal strengths and weaknesses (and comparative statements about competition)
- a statement setting out long-term objectives (specific to growth, financial return, etc.) and how they will be achieved
- next year's specific objectives
- a plan of timed, specific marketing activity (across the marketing mix), showing what will be done, in what order, and allowing co-ordination of the different elements in a way that links exactly to what achievements are planned
- a link with intended longer term, i.e. outline plans for subsequent years (typically three or five in all, though some heavy industries need longer, and certain Japanese companies talk about one hundred year plans, and mean it!)
- identification of the priorities for action linked to opportunities and action specified (here it may be as important to say what will not be done, as to say what will, many organisations end up trying to do too much and, as a result, do not do anything sufficiently well to guarantee success).

   *Note:*   *The important thing here is to regard this as a rolling process, i.e. to work with a progressively changing situation, updating, revising and accommodating change in a dynamic market place so that progress continues smoothly, rather than suddenly having to think about things as change dictates.*

Finally, three aspects are surely particularly important in discussing planning:

1. *Market focus*: No one involved in the process can afford to be divorced in any way from the market. This links to planning, research, observation and involvement and demands an ongoing process if, at any time, you are going to be able to say, genuinely, 'I am in touch with the market'. It does not always happen. A question the author sometimes ask participants on sales courses is: 'How often do members of the non-sales staff accompany you in the field to meet customers and observe the sales interface?' There are exceptions, of course, but many say it happens rarely, and some that it never happens. There can surely be no excuse for this; innovations are likely to be more difficult if attempted in a vacuum.

2. T*ime*: The pressures of day-to-day activity usually make it difficult to find any 'thinking time'. Yet progress will not be made unless time is set aside, specifically, for working through the possibilities and this may, in turn, mean that particular combinations of people get together for this purpose. What we are identifying here is a priority by any reasonable measure, but one that may be difficult to make happen. It is the sort of thing that is threatened by the dominance of the urgent over the important.

    Success here will not come, or come readily, unless there is sufficient time made available. Time management is a core skill. It affects performance so much and is particularly crucial when creativity needs to be brought to bear. Time management can be directed simply at sorting day-to-day productivity, but it is most important in allowing concentration on priorities. In this regard it is a differentiating factor, actually influencing which companies do better than their less well organised competitors.

3. S*ystem*: If time is to be found for this kind of process, then, of course, some sort of system is needed. Many companies have regular meetings to consider new proposals. Finding time for them may be problem enough, but more is necessary. If more radical and innovative issues are to be progressed then time must be found for this too. This time may need organising separately from more routine gatherings, otherwise there is a danger that it is relegated to the bottom of the agenda and pushed out by more immediately pressing matters. Something more than good intentions is necessary here if important matters are to be progressed in parallel with everyday (and important!) issues.

    If this is done, and open-minded discussion is allowed to take place, then there is a greater chance that really new initiatives will result and planning can be moved away from working within the status quo.

**Warning**

It may be obvious, given what has been said above, but a lack of clear planning can sound the death knell for even the best product or service. If you do not know where you are going, any road will do. And the wrong road can lead to failure.

# Marketing strategy

## Introduction

Developing marketing strategies is a key part of the marketing planning process (see MARKETING PLANNING). This section describes the role of strategies in making marketing plans and their implementation successful.

The terminology is important here so, at the risk of becoming pedantic, it is important to make clear that:

- the objective is the *desired result* in the market place
- the strategy is a *course of action* designed to achieve that result.

The strategy must focus effort, co-ordinate action and exploit the identified strengths of the organisation (and avoid waste on peripheral activities).

The selection of strategies need not be mutually exclusive; more than one may work well with another. However, there is a real danger of trying to do too much, on too broad a front, and this may well lead to little or nothing being well executed.

The main objective/strategic options open to any company are to:

1. *Increase existing share of the market*: e.g. through the strategies of market segmentation, seeking new applications, using different imprints for differing segments.
2. *Expand existing markets*: e.g. by increasing frequency of product purchase, selling through new outlets, increasing promotion.
3. *Develop new markets for existing products*: Expanding the range of segments dealt with, e.g. through overseas expansion.
4. *Develop new products in new markets*: (A high risk route) by diversification or technological development – this is what is happening in some businesses affected by computer and IT innovations.
5. *Increase the profitability of increasing business*: Improving 'product quality', raising price, revising sales systems and improving productivity.

The brief examples quoted here with each main strategic option illustrate various possibilities and highlight the link between objectives and strategy.

This area must be detailed clearly in the plan; beyond that the *tactical* working of that plan must reflect and fine-tune the intentions and make things work day-to-day in the market, and in response to the market.

# Media planning

## Introduction

The term refers to the task of deciding the most cost-effective mix to use in advertising from the considerable range of media available. This includes decisions about related fields (which newspaper(s)), between unrelated fields (television or newspapers) and about the very wide range of other media possibilities: from book matches to the side of the space shuttle, from sponsored litter bins to the backs of bus tickets.

Media planning is complex. The media planner needs to know not only what the options are (in terms of details like the total readership of a magazine, the different categories of people represented and what results seem to have been achieved from it in the past), but also their cost and relative performance. Not least, recommendations must bear in mind what is appropriate for the organisation, the product and the customers involved.

See also ADVERTISING and ADVERTISING AGENCY.

## Warning

For small companies (and sometimes larger ones) there is a particular danger: that of selecting a particular medium on a subjective one-off basis. This happens, for instance, when a trade magazine telephones saying that they are doing a special feature on your product area and *all your competitors are taking space.* If this is said, and a 'special' price quoted (which may well not be all that special), it can be enough to produce a decision which is only superficially and momentarily sensible. Other media might suit much better.

**Definition:** *Merchandising*

See DISPLAY AND MERCHANDISING.

# Mission statements

**Introduction**

This sounds like the ultimate piece of American jargon: a device of no real substance. In fact, it has real value.

The only point of any planning activity is to help ensure that the business goes better than it would without planning. Everything done, therefore, must have a practical edge. Some aspects of planning may seem, at first, somewhat esoteric. Much of the jargon of marketing originates in America, and there is a danger of writing it off as having little to do with actually running the business.

One such phrase is *mission statement*. It describes the purpose and key objective of an organisation. Such a statement is useful to both thinking and communication (and subsequently to creating and/or maintaining attitudes throughout an organisation).

Too often people believe that a company's mission is obvious or 'goes without saying'. However, what may be obvious to top management may not permeate the organisation and generate shared company values and styles which, in turn, help prompt the right kind of action. A simplistic statement, such as 'Our goal is to sell good quality widgets and make a profit', may do little for the business. But a properly constructed mission statement, one which considers the many dimensions of a company's relationship with its environment and which includes time, purpose and direction – all with a customer focus – can be of real practical value. There is then a clear, and common, view of why the company is in business, with what resources the business will be managed, and towards what ends.

Not least it prompts ongoing consideration of key questions:

- What is our business?
- Who are our customers?
- What represents value to the customers?
- What will our future business be?

Much of the detail that a company must deal with and manage is likely to be based on the answers to such fundamental questions; indeed on their continuous review and update. The mission of an organisation is shaped essentially from five key elements:

1.  *History of the organisation*: Every organisation has a history of aims, policies and accomplishments. In reaching for future purpose, it must build on key elements of its past (instant radical switches of activity may simply be impractical).
2.  *Current preferences of the management and owners*: These two could, of course, be the same; or in opposition. Although important, this aspect should not predominate to the exclusion of a sufficiently realistic market focus.
3.  *Environmental considerations*: Those that define the main opportunities and threats that must be taken into account and which influence the purpose of the organisation.
4.  *Resources of the organisation*: These will make certain missions possible and rule out others, at least in the short term. The term applies in its widest interpretation and includes everything from people and their expertise and competencies, to, of course, financial considerations.
5.  *Existing distinctive competence*: Simply wanting to do something is clearly not enough; the ability to do it must be there too. It is important to be very hard-nosed in this area, though competencies can be changed over time.

Any mission statement should also have a definite market focus. It should define:

*   the customer groups that will be served
*   the customer needs that will be met
*   the technology and processes that will satisfy these needs.

Such a market focus is more important than a simple product one (though both are clearly inter-related); marketing insists we see the business as a customer-satisfying process, not as a product-producing one. Turning the mission into concrete goals and an action plan facilitates all aspects of planning and subsequent implementation and control.

# New product development

**Introduction**

In consumer-products marketing it is well documented that nine out of ten new products launched fail within two years. First we might ask what a new product is. There are very few new products, but many new versions of things. When facsimile machines arrived on the scene they were a genuinely new way of communicating (and having shares in companies making telex machines was thereafter not a good idea). More often a 'new product' is a new version of something, perhaps with good, tangible advantages; perhaps only repackaged or with 'cosmetic' changes.

Whatever its nature the launch of a new product is an important event for any marketing department. It needs careful planning and execution. And the statistics are not favourable.

The first job is the creative one of coming up with a new product concept. If the newness of this is minor, but the mass marketing of it will be expensive then it is a major decision. If it is a major capital item – a new airliner – then it may imply years of research and development and a substantial marketing programme running in concert.

Even simple ideas we now take for granted bear some thought. Take the warm, waistcoat-like garments or 'gilets' that have been fashionable for some years. Can you imagine someone walking into their boss's office and saying something like: 'I've got this great idea for a new style of warm winter jacket – with no sleeves'. Would it provoke instant acceptance or a laugh?

When a new product is agreed then detailed project management takes over. It must be launched in a way that co-ordinates many, and often disparate, factors. For example, when an advertising campaign breaks Production must be on top of the job of supplying, products must be in stock in retailers and other communication (say press coverage) must be on time. Any mismatch, such as a customer being told that a shop has not heard of it, can cause problems, at worst failure.

Sometimes, especially with consumer products, *test marketing* is used. This typically takes the form of a limited launch (often in a geographical region covered by its own commercial television channel for products advertised that way) to test the water. Costs are kept low until success seems indicated; then the launch can go national, or international. The competition will follow whatever is done closely and aim to minimise its success if possible. Customers may be suspicious, fickle or simply uninterested – the number of hazards are legion.

Research will often be used in the early stages (see MARKET RESEARCH), and the whole process links closely to factors such as branding (see BRANDING). In some industries launching a new product is a regular event; in others a rare one. Once launched it becomes part of the range, needing regular marketing activity to develop it and keep it successful (see also PRODUCT LIFE-CYCLE).

New product development and launch incorporates many aspects of the whole marketing process focused on the one task. Success is never guaranteed, but the rewards of getting it right are high.

---

**Definition:** *Niche marketing*

A market niche is simply the smallest, most focused, level of market segment. So a computer company might target people who need a computer and work at home: a market segment. They may then focus beyond that on those within the segment who have specific needs, say for a colour printer and sophisticated graphic software for work in design: this is a market niche.

See also SEGMENTATION

# Overseas marketing

**Introduction**

The fourth 'P' of the marketing mix (along with product, price and presentation – see MARKETING MIX) is place. Generally speaking the more widely a product can be distributed geographically the more of it will be sold. There used to be a much quoted maxim – 'export or die' – and certainly a nation's balance of payments is made healthier if exports are high. In the UK, despite all the exhortation to export, some 90 per cent of total exports (by value) is sold by a few hundred organisations within the country, though historically those companies that have taken overseas opportunities seriously have increased business as a result.

All the principles of marketing apply overseas. Without going into too much detail, electing to define two areas of activity as follows indicates the scope involved:

1. *Export marketing*: This is essentially selling goods to overseas customers, often through distributors or agents, but doing so from a base in your base market.

   *Note:* *This is an area that demands specialist knowledge of such things as export documentation, shipping, insurance, credit control, etc., as well as marketing.*

2. *International marketing*: This implies a greater involvement in the overseas territories – everything from setting up subsidiaries to joint ventures and, in some businesses, local manufacture. (The complexities here can become considerable, with components being sourced from several different locations around the world, assembled in one or more main centres and then distributed to and sold in many markets.)

Throughout industry, some companies sell what they produce worldwide; others tailor the product to individual markets – even something as simple as a chocolate bar may have many different recipes and flavours for each of many different markets. This applies to many aspects of a product: cars may need change to meet local safety standards, books may need translating, electrical products may have to work with different voltages, etc. It is simply arrogant to assume no change is needed, so marketing logically demands consideration of such options and adaptations being made as necessary.

The marketing principle of 'knowing your customer' is clearly paramount in overseas markets where people, culture, customs, etc. may be very different. Such differences will not only potentially affect details relating to the product (e.g. a colour may be popular in one country and regarded as unlucky in another) but also the manner of doing business. Here such things as the prevailing practice regarding negotiation, business ethics or time scale may all be different. Even a name – of a company or product – may need careful checking; what sounds catchy in English may be lewd in German or Urdu. (For example, it is unlikely that certain overseas products, such as *Sweat*, a Japanese drink, or *Nora Knackers*, a Norwegian crispbread, would do very well in the UK.) Another key factor of marketing overseas is the increased commitment necessary; people, resources and money are all spread more widely.

If success is to be had, it needs an appropriate commitment in these terms. It also demands that operational factors respect different geographical conditions. Some markets – France, say – are small for certain traditional English products (like marmalade). Others – South-East Asia – are largely English-speaking, so will buy more English language books and magazines than, say, Taiwan. Distance is important too. Singapore may be five or six thousand miles away, but customers there are no different from anywhere else; they want to be looked after. There is no substitute for personal contact. If you want to operate overseas, you must go overseas. Not only can more be done face to face, but physical presence in many territories is read as commitment.

Again this is an area that illustrates the dynamic nature of marketing. The world itself is changing as we watch; new markets are opening up and, at the same time, other markets may contract, for reasons as varied as change of government to natural disaster.

# *Packaging*

**Introduction**

The packaging of any product is often an inherent part of the product and some is enormously distinctive (e.g. the Coca Cola bottle). Certainly, how a product looks is very much part of its total image and, if it is good, will strengthen its appeal and saleability.

In a sense the packaging is a form of advertisement. There are also more practical considerations to it, such as security and protection in transit and ease of stacking neatly. See also PHYSICAL DISTRIBUTION.

**Definition:** *Pareto's Law*

This, more commonly known as the 80/20 rule, stems from the observation of the eighteenth-century Italian economist after whom it is named, that 80 per cent of the wealth of Florence was in the hands of 20 per cent of its people.

The ratio seems to hold good for many business situations: from the view, in time management, that 80 per cent of a manager's results come from just 20 per cent of their time and effort, to ratios linked more tightly to marketing. For example, that 80 per cent of revenue comes from 20 per cent of the customer base; and the same with profit.

The ratio is a sufficiently reliable guide to be used as a tangible part of marketing and sales analysis (see KEY ACCOUNTS).

# Party plan marketing

**Introduction**

Another specialised approach to marketing which is very successful for some, but not widely appropriate or used.

This is a specialist marketing approach, used only by a small number of companies. The best-known example is Tupperware, which makes specialist kitchenware and sells via parties in the home. The technique consists of a company team who recruit people in the home, who in turn invite friends and others to a social gathering at which products are displayed and described. It creates a genuine social event and thus does attract attendees. The householder who provides the venue and assembles the 'audience' is rewarded, either with money or with the possibility of buying goods at a discount.

Other products sold this way include lingerie and children's books. In this latter case the main exponent is a company called Usborne Books which sells semi-educational books, very successfully, to parents of young, often pre-school, children.

This is a good example of creative marketing, really seeking out and finding (creating?) new ways of marketing. What matters is that it works for those who do it, not that every organisation should be able to do it.

# *Physical distribution*

**Introduction**

Marketing and sales create demand, and the process of making sure goods get to the customer on time and in perfect condition is termed 'physical distribution'. Physical distribution management is the integration of two or more activities for the purpose of planning, implementing and controlling the efficient flow of raw materials, in-process inventory and finished goods from point of origin to point of sale and consumption.

These activities may include, but are not limited to, customer service, demand-forecasting, distribution communications, inventory control, material-handling, order-processing, service support, plant and warehouse site selection, procurement, packaging, return-goods handling, transportation, warehousing and storage. From this list it will be obvious how closely sales and physical distribution should work together to ensure maximum efficiency in achieving results and maintaining reliability in meeting orders. Each link in the chain between initial enquiry, order-placing, manufacturing or goods from stock process, packaging, transport and delivery to the customer must be under constant scrutiny or costs and prices will quickly get out of control. And customer service is always paramount.

Customer service is clearly inherently linked to marketing and may come under the control of an aspect of it – the sales department, say. Other factors, in part an element of physical distribution, have a dual role. Packaging has to protect the goods, meet additional specifications such as safe and convenient stacking on a display, and may also perform a promotional function; the pack is a mobile advertisement (and a purveyor of information); this dual rôle applies to a range of factors from product labelling to display material.

In most organisations the management of the physical distribution process will not be directly run by marketing; the overlap and the importance of this area to marketing success, however, are clear. Something arriving late and damaged will not begin to persuade the customer to buy again, and creates administration problems and costs. Something arriving promptly, safely and in a way which adds to the attractiveness of the whole deal, well might.

---

**Warning**

Physical distribution may – sensibly – operate at a little distance from marketing and not be directly controlled by it. Nevertheless the two are inextricably bound up. If physical distribution fails, if the product arrives damaged or not at all, then marketing suffers very directly and the impact on customers and on their resulting view of the company may be long lived.

---

**Definition:** *Point of sale*

This term refers specifically to the place where ultimate sale takes place. Thus a manufacturer sells biscuits, say, to a wholesaler who sells them to retailers; only when a customer picks up a packet in a shop is this described as occurring at the 'point of sale'. It is an area manufacturers set out to influence in various ways, with promotions that are evident or finalised at the point of sale, or through the way the retail environment is made attractive to customers.

See both PROMOTION and MERCHANDISING.

---

**Definition:** *Positioning*

See BRANDING (and within that section: *Brand positioning*).

# Press relations

### Introduction

Press relations is a very specific form of public relations (see PUBLIC RELATIONS for an overview of this topic) that can pay dividends in building a positive image and helping put over promotional messages. Unlike an advertisement, though, there is no guarantee of what will be said as a result of initiatives taken. The press will bring their own thinking to bear, not simply help uncritically. Having said that, there is no reason to feel that the press will be critical, and if there are good things to say about an organisation or product then the resultant press coverage can be a valuable part of the overall promotional mix.

Though personal contact with journalists and others is important, much can be achieved through the *press release* – a structured, written communication to the press intended to be the basis of a story or press mention. These lead the vital search for comment, review and news about an organisation in the media.

Despite the fact that control over the results is to a degree uncertain – a press release may be ignored or given the wrong slant when it is written up – the opportunities here are legion: press, TV, radio and newspapers and magazines of every description (some specialising, of course, in topics that link to the company's special area of interest).

Press releases can be in the form of routine mentions or of more particular stories, but in both cases much of the impact of any sort of material is cumulative. Customers will sometimes comment, 'we seem to see mentions of the firm pretty regularly' but have difficulty remembering the exact context of what was said, or more likely written. To achieve this cumulative impact, the PR people need to be constantly on the look-out for opportunities of gaining a mention.

Even routine matters, perhaps the appointment of a new member of staff or a move of offices, may be written up and contribute to the whole process. This is particularly so with regard to trade press which has a focus on specific industries, and many journals of this sort are full of such, often inconsequential, news – but it helps the cumulative process of keeping a name visible. It must all be thought of, done regularly, and done right. While some routine stories will get a mention, particularly if the company is well known, news means just what it says!

While it may be of interest internally that the firm has 25 staff, inhabits an eighteenth-century mansion or is reorganising, a journalist will tend to find it difficult to imagine readers starry-eyed with excitement as they read it in their newspaper or journal. A company must find something with more of an element of news in it; it may be genuinely different, it may be a first comment on something, but it must truly have something of real interest about it.

If a company, or its spokesperson, becomes known as a source of good comment, stories and articles, then press contacts will start to come to *them*, and the whole process may gain continuity and momentum. In addition, a number of events can be linked to press and public relations activity. For example, both social events and exhibitions and demonstrations fulfil this role, creating something more than simply the news item for the press to get their teeth into. Such events must be appropriate to the nature of the organisation, product and occasion. Some industries engage in considerable hype (think of a film première); in others their very nature calls for a lower-key approach.

The press release that carries information of the type discussed here is a specialist document, which has to be put together with care. If the detail of this is important to you an example, the press release to be sent out on the publication of this book, is shown in Figure 7. Whether this will be picked up and quoted by the press remains to be seen, but as an example of the kind of release that may generate comment it is reasonably typical.

It should be noted that specialist skills are involved here. If a company spokesperson is to be interviewed on radio, say, then it pays to take some time to check out the process. Even the style of writing appropriate for a press release may not be easy for everyone.

Lastly, it should be remembered that sometimes (one hopes, rarely) the job of public relations is to combat bad publicity. Whether the company is at fault, or whether it is just rumour, care is needed to set the record straight and get the image-generating process back on track.

Creating the right image may be a long, hard process; once achieved it is essentially fragile – losing it or letting it become tarnished may take but a moment, and may be difficult to recover from in the future.

# ICSA Publishing *PRESS RELEASE \* PRESS RELEASE*

ICSA Publishing Ltd
Campus 400
Maylands Avenue
Hemel Hempstead
Hertfordshire
HP2 7EZ, England

Tel: 01442 881900
Fax: 01442 252544 Telex: 82445

**Would you like a review copy?**
Contact Abbi Quinn
Tel: 01442 882247
Email: abbi_quinn@prenhall.co.uk
Or FAX BACK the form overleaf

## *Question:* **What is the key aspect of any organisation's success in the market place?**
## *Answer:* **Marketing**

But if you're still unsure what marketing is, then let this new title in the One Stop series, **One Stop Marketing**, answer all your questions

Marketing matters. There is more to marketing than meets the eye: it is more than just advertising or selling. Rather, it is a whole approach to business, designed to give it direction and ensure profitability.

In **One Stop Marketing** (£14.95, June) *Patrick Forsyth* provides a practical introduction to marketing, demystifiying the process, explaining individual techniques and demonstrating how the different elements of marketing interact. He also relates marketing to the wider context of other business functions and to the outside world of competition, markets and customers.

<u>If you would like a copy for review, fax back the form overleaf</u>

Whether you're new to the marketing environment or merely want a brief overview of what it is all about, **One Stop Marketing** will give you a wealth of information on all aspects in an accessible style and format, introducing and explaining key concepts as they appear.

**Patrick Forsyth** runs Touchstone Training and Consultancy which works in areas of marketing, sales, communication and management skills. He has more than twenty years' experience running both in-company and public training. He writes regularly on marketing matters in management journals, and is the author of a number of successful management books on topics such as report writing, presentation skills and time management as well as marketing.

The **One Stop** series provides essential information for anyone involved in running a business. The books in the series offer you facts and guidance about running your business legally, efficiently and profitably. All the titles are written in a clear, user-friendly style using practical models, examples, cases and checklists.
*See over the page for a complete listing of titles*

**One Stop Marketing** by *Patrick Forsyth* is published by ICSA Publishing at £14.95

The Official Publishing Company of the Institute of Chartered Secretaries and Administrators

Registered Office: The Institute of Chartered Secretaries and Administrators, 16 Park Crescent, London W1N 4AH. Registration: England & Wales 1576690

*Figure 7  Example of press release*

# Pricing

**Introduction**

Price is a major marketing variable (one of the classic three 'P's of the marketing mix), and how it is dealt with has a direct bearing on how successful, or not, a product will be in the market. And – very important – on how much profit it will generate. First let us look at some of the main principles involved in pricing policy for any product. However, before that, it is important to recognise that price and image are inextricably linked. In fact the product, its price and its image are viewed together by the ultimate customer, for any product.

What customers want, above all, is value for money. This applies whatever the product. It does *not* follow that they want the cheapest product available. This is a point well made by the apocryphal story of one of the first men on the moon. He was asked what he thought about in the last few seconds of the countdown before the rocket took off on its historic voyage. He thought for a moment and said: 'I remembered that there were 500,000 working parts in the machine below me and that, in every case, the contract had gone to the lowest bidder'. There are certainly situations where the perception of price does not boost confidence. Things can be too cheap (a word so easily associated with 'nasty'). So it is not just the Rolls-Royce name that speaks of quality, it is the price tag. If it cost the same as a Mini then there would be less kudos in owning one.

But what people think of the price is only part of the picture. There are four basic criteria that form part of any decision to set a price. They are:

1. *Cost-based pricing*: This is sometimes called the accountancy approach and is based on taking the cost of a product (all the costs, including an allocation for overheads) and adding a margin for profit to produce a selling price.
2. *Market demand-based pricing*: This looks at price from the point of view of demand. Classically, high demand means that a higher price can be achieved; a lower demand means the reverse. It is the price/demand relationship that gives rise to the description of price elasticity; in other words, demand varies depending on how price is set.

123

3. *Competition-based pricing*: This, clearly, relates a particular company's price to the price of similar products in the market place. Taking this view allows price to be set intentionally higher, lower, or on a par with the competition. Depending on where the level is set links to the positioning of the product – how it is set against others in terms of price and other factors.

4. *Marketing-based pricing*: Only this includes the marketing view. Its aim is to ensure that price is set in such a way as to produce value satisfaction in customers. Such perceptions can be influenced by:

   • all aspects of the company, its product and service
   • status: endorsements by opinion leaders, exclusivity or promotion
   • price barriers that may operate in a segment.

   This involves what may not be easy judgements. It may be easy to overvalue, and thus overprice, your product, though it is also possible to do the reverse.

Note that the four methodologies described above are not alternatives. Elements of each viewpoint need to be included in the overall thinking and if one is underrated then the price set may be out of kilter and not work well in the market, either losing profit or sales.

High and low price may be used strategically. For example, skimming pricing is setting a high price, perhaps when there is little competition, to maximise sales from initial purchases. This happens in, amongst others, the computer and other fast-changing technological equipment markets. Similarly, penetration pricing aims to increases sales by setting a lower and highly competitive price, thereby maximising profit only through higher volume sales.

## How it seems

Perception of price in the market is not an entirely rational thing; indeed consumers even find it difficult to recall the price they have paid for many products they have bought. For example, price barriers operate around particular figures and give rise to much-seen prices such as £9.99 and £14.99 (and also in some fields barriers such as £1,000 and £10,000). These may not seem so different from £10 and £15 and are not! But people like them: all the research done seems to show that such pricing has greater appeal and sells more products than the round-figure price. (It also reduces staff pilferage in retailers as, say, a £10 note necessitates the till being opened and change being given.) The moral is to forget the logic; it matters less why this happens than that it is something to use.

Attitudes to such factors, however, can and do change. Marks & Spencer is currently reverting largely to round-figure pricing; maybe though, such attitudes are, in part, influenced by fashion and for a while the obvious ease for customers of a straightforward approach will be the norm before another approach is tried.

## Increasing sales

Price is used in a variety of ways to assist marketing and ensure, or increase, sales. The classic example of this is price promotion. This takes various forms, e.g.:

- two for the price of one
- discounts for early decision
- special offers
- quantity discounts
- the 'sales'.

Two other methods are worth noting. The first is the practice in some product areas of quoting an attractive basic price and making other things – sometimes essential things – extra. Car manufacturers do this, and the author was recently shocked to see just how much essential leads, etc. added to the cost of computer equipment. Of course, a competitive position may be to do the reverse and promote things on an inclusive basis.

Secondly, it should be noted that in some product areas price is high because it is linked to image. Fashion products are like this, and both the customer and the provider know, yet people still buy the 'classy' brands. There are many examples, with products ranging from Filofax to certain brands of trainers carrying a premium price. Indeed, in FMCG product areas generally, it is rare to find a brand leader amongst the cheapest products. The logic is clear: high price allows more promotional spend which in turn sells more goods and the cycle continues.

One last point, in what is actually an area where there is much detail for marketing people to worry about: a new jargon phrase, 'complexity pricing', has recently crept into the marketing vocabulary. In some areas – mobile telephones are a good example – options of supplier, price and service become so complicated that consumers actually have no idea whether they are getting a reasonable deal or not. There are those who would advocate this as a desirable tactic when competitive pressure is particularly tight.

# Product life-cycle

**Introduction**

This is a classic concept of the marketing process and it is important to be clear just what it implies.

Products do not go on for ever. Some are here today and gone tomorrow: consider fashion products, pop records or newspapers. Of course, others last a long while, and we can probably all think of brand names that we view as ubiquitous, indeed that our parents viewed in the same way: how long have Bovril, Persil or Black Magic been around? Some fade away; others have a more dramatic demise – witness the way in which the advent of the fax virtually destroyed the market for telex machines in a very short time.

The product life-cycle (see Figure 8) goes through five distinct stages: introduction, growth, maturity, decline, phase out. Each of these is worth a separate comment.

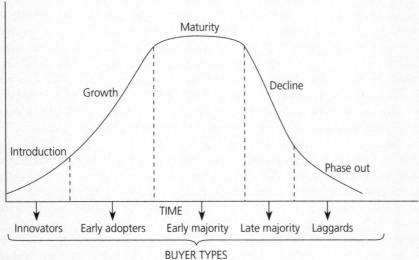

*Figure 8 Product life-cycle*

1.  *Introduction*: This may involve a slow start, or up-front investment, or both.
2.  *Growth*: Market acceptance and purchase speed up, profitability grows and the scene must be set to secure a place for the product in the longer term.
3.  *Maturity*: Sales growth may slow down, but it can be the period of greatest profitability. However, it may take work to keep a product at this stage and there is always the threat of gradual decline setting in.
4.  *Decline*: Eventually this is inevitable, though decline of revenue and profit may be made gradual if the right action is taken.
5.  *Phase out*: The product finally dies and must be withdrawn as additional efforts to maintain sales can become self-defeating.

The speed and slope of the classic product life-cycle curve, illustrated in Figure 7, together with an indication of how different kinds of people take up the really new products, varies a great deal depending on circumstances and the item in question.

## Actively using the product life-cycle

The key point above is the last: marketing must actively work the product life-cycle, and aim to speed growth, extend maturity and slow decline – all in order to maximise revenue and profit. Good ongoing sales from an existing product range are surely dependent on this sort of view being reflected in action.

This can be illustrated by describing the (possible, more likely exaggerated) future of this book. This might first have been published in hardback, then in a book club edition, then in paperback. In due course it could be revised, appear in a second edition and repeat the cycle of various editions. It could also be translated into, say, two other languages, extending its life still further. As well as the second edition, an extended version might be produced, made possible by the addition of a number of illustrated case studies. And as it would then become a work of reference, it could be issued on a CD-ROM format, and even, in another form, in a pack with an accompanying video.

All this might take some time, and could still not begin to exhaust the possibilities. Such possibilities, of course, are inherent from the beginning. The original marketing plan for the title should begin to explore such possibilities, not least because they can change the viability of the whole project.

Any product can be thought about and developed in this way. The product will, by its nature, dictate the possibilities, but the action will aim to use the life-cycle concept systematically to explore and extend the possibilities for longer life and increased sales.

This is a process that encompasses what is called product development, which is so often a process of evolution rather than revolution. A number of changes, perhaps minor or significant in their own right, ultimately lead to more radical development. (See also NEW PRODUCT DEVELOPMENT.)

# *Product range*

**Introduction**

This term can be used in a very general way, simply to imply that a number of different products are sold by one organisation. This is the case with most organisations, though there are exceptions (Wrigleys sell nothing but chewing gum).

Different products may not only be different in nature, but occupy different positions and rôles within the range. Some may have been around a while; others may be new and either may contribute more or less to the profitability of the organisation.

Marketing people may review the product range by using a form of analysis such as that in Figure 9.

This analysis is first to categorise the products, then to allow decisions about their future (e.g. whether to develop or drop them) to be made. The chart shown on the next page is a simplified version of the concept first developed by the Boston Consulting Group and known as the Boston Matrix.

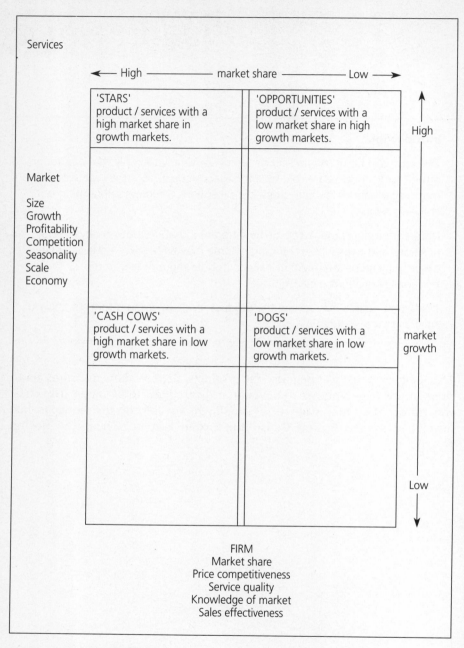

*Figure 9  Product range analysis*

# Promotion

## Introduction

Again there is a problem with marketing's imprecise use of terms: promotion is used both as an umbrella term for all sorts of advertising and promotional activity, and also as a sub-section of that, i.e. sales promotion, which is a miscellany of techniques ranging from competitions to shop window stickers.

In this section the term 'promotion' is used to provide an overview; other sections investigate particular techniques in more detail.

Promotion is, for many, the most interesting part of marketing; certainly it is the most visible, with elements of it – advertisements, posters and so on – all around us. It is also a very important element. As the quotation which starts this book makes clear, no business will be done even by the producer of the best product or service if no one knows of its existence.

Promotion is not, however, just a vehicle of information; it must be persuasive, and it must differentiate. Remember, potential customers may see the range of goods offered by competitors as somewhat similar. This is true of many areas, e.g. cars – consider how many very similar makes exist in each category – or fax machines, or hotels, or washing machines, etc. To a large extent it is the promotional elements that allow people to make a judgement about what, from all that is available, is right for them.

## What is being promoted?

Branding is mentioned a number of times through this text. It is worth a mention here. The brand name is usually a name given to a product rather than a company (though they can be the same, e.g. McDonalds). Some companies have strong brand names – one thinks first of FMCG products such as Coca Cola, Persil, Bovril, but also of BMW, IBM and Penguin Books and of industrial firms like ICI, which also has consumer sub-brands such as Dulux paint. Other companies could cultivate strong images, though it would need effort and time. This does not, or should not, rule it out.

There are companies which use the company name for all their brands, e.g. Virgin, with airlines, records, even bridal wear shops, and others which use many brand names and leave the company name in the background, e.g. Lever Brothers. As ever with marketing approaches there is no one way and certainly no one right way.

In reading on through this section on promotion it will be useful to keep in mind exactly what you need to promote in your organisation, as this is clearly the most important question.

## The promotion mix

Promotion comprises a range of different elements; mix is the right word and the various promotional techniques themselves are not mutually exclusive. They are often used together or in various combinations. Each works in a rather different way, principally in how directly and in what way it relates to the market. Figure 10 shows the different distance at which each operates from the potential customer; it is this that characterises the different rôle which various techniques play. It should be noted that the customer can be defined here in any way you wish – as the consumer, or as someone along the chain.

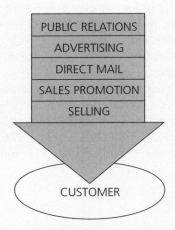

*Figure 10  The mix of persuasive communications*

Promotion does not act in a vacuum; it must relate to the way a potential purchaser moves progressively towards actual purchase, and act to change the attitudes of the target audience to whom it is directed. With many products it is not just purchase that is the aim, but repeat purchase, as when a householder re-supplies with, say, the same brand of soap. Various objectives may be set, e.g. persuading a customer to:

134

- try a product
- buy more, or more often
- extend the use of the product, thus buying more (e.g. cornflakes for supper)
- trust the brand name, buying more across a range of products.

The stages in the buying process move from a situation where the consumer has no knowledge of the company or product (and is usually referred to as 'unaware') to one where they are, for the time being at least, regular users. Each stage represents a tangible change and the process is worth examining sequentially.

1. *Unawareness awareness*: This is the stage during which a buyer moves from no knowledge of a product towards a position where they know about it, or at least of its existence. The buyer's attitude is almost passive and their major need is to be informed. Promotion is targeted at:

   - introducing a concept
   - telling the buyer that something more specific exists
   - creating an automatic association between the needs area and the product.

2. *Awareness interest*: This is a movement from a passive stage to an active stage of attention. The buyer will have their curiosity aroused by the product's newness, appearance or concept. Their response, however, can be conscious or subconscious. Promotional objectives are to:

   - gain their attention through the message
   - create interest (motivation)
   - provide a succinct summary of the product (information).

   (At this stage, aspects of the whole mix begin to get the buyer saying, 'I must watch out for this, it seems worth checking out'.)

3. *Interest evaluation*: The buyer will first consider the effect of the product on their personal motivation (life-style, image, needs, circumstances, etc.). Then they will look at the effect on external factors. They will pass through a process of reasoning, analysing the arguments and looking for advantages. Depending upon their needs, they might look for more information or validation of an initial impression. Through promotion, an attempt is made to:

   - create a situation that encourages the buyer to start this phase of reasoning
   - discover and focus on the buyer's relevant needs
   - segment and target buyers according to the needs requirements.

4. *Evaluation trial*: This is a key movement from a mental state of evaluation to a positive action of trial. The buyer's basic requirement is for a suitable opportunity to use the product. Promotional objectives are to:

   - clearly identify usage opportunities
   - suggest usage when these opportunities occur.

   In other words to encourage first purchase. ('This does look good – I'll buy it.')

5. *Trial usage*: The buyer will take this step if the trial has been successful. The objectives of the promotion are to:

   - provide reminders of key elements, such as brand, image advantages, etc.
   - emphasise the success and satisfaction
   - remind the buyer of usage opportunities and provide supporting proof via third-party references.

6. *Repeat usage*: This is the final objective for promotion. When a buyer moves from occasional usage to constant usage, he or she will have moved into a state where selection of the product is automatic. The objectives are now simpler and are to:

   - maintain the climate that has led to satisfaction
   - maintain an acceptable image
   - keep confirming the key qualities of the product.

The above sequence dissects the process in detail and, though the customer may not be aware of proceeding quite so consciously through the process – and indeed may make rapid and seemingly instinctive leaps along the way – this sequence is real and is what promotion must influence.

The promotional elements creating the above effect and progression can be comprised of any combination of the overall mix: everything from the effect of a small detail (such as a sticker in a shop window) to a major campaign (posters on the London Underground). With this in mind marketing can utilise and deploy the separate and individual techniques, making them work to achieve exactly what is wanted. It is important to bear in mind, when implementing these techniques, that the effect of each is different, and that it is difficult to separate each individual impact. A person's image of an organisation is the net and cumulative effect of everything they see and hear about it.

See also PROMOTIONAL BUDGET and the individual headings referring to the various promotional techniques.

# *Promotional budgets*

**Introduction**

There are several approaches to the complex issue of setting the promotional budget. This section reviews the approaches and suggests how a rational decision can be made in this vexed area.

The main approaches to setting a promotional budget are:

1. *Percentage of sales*: To take a fixed percentage, based usually on forecast sales, relies on the questionable assumption that there is always a direct relationship between promotional expenditure and sales. It assumes, for example, that if increased sales of 10 per cent are forecast, a 10 per cent increase in promotional effort will also be required. This may or may not be realistic and depends on many external factors. The most traditional and easiest approach, it is also probably the least effective.

2. *Competitive parity approach*: This involves spending the same amount on promotion as competitive firms, or maintaining a proportional expenditure of average industry appropriation, or using an identical percentage of gross sales revenue as other similar organisations. The assumption is that in this way market share will be maintained. However, the competition may be aiming at a slightly different sector and including competition in the broadest sense is no help. If you can form a view of competitive/industry activity it may be useful, but the danger of this approach is that competitors' spending represents the 'collective wisdom' of the industry, and the blind may end up leading the blind!

It is important to remember that competitive expenditure cannot be more than an indication of the budget that should be established. In terms of strategy it is entirely possible that expenditure should be either considerably greater than a competitor's – to drive them out – or, perhaps for other reasons, a lot less.

Remember that no two firms pursue identical objectives from an identical base line of resources, market standing, etc., and that it is fallacious to assume that all competitors will spend equal or proportional amounts of money with exactly the same level of efficiency.

3. *Combining percentage of sales and competitive parity* (i.e. 1 and 2): This is a slightly more comprehensive approach to setting the budget, but still does not overcome the problems inherent in each individual method. It does, however, recognise the need for maintaining profitability and takes into account the likely impact of competitive expenditure.

4. *What is affordable?*: This method appears to be based on the premise that if spending something is right, but the optimum amount cannot objectively be decided upon, whatever money is available will do.
   Look at:

   • what is available after all the other costs have been accounted for, i.e. premises, staff, selling expenses, etc.
   • the cash situation in the business as a whole
   • the revenue forecast.

   In some companies advertising and promotion are left to share out the tail-end of the budget; more expenditure being considered analogous with lower profits. In others, more expenditure on promotion might lead to more sales at marginal cost which in turn would lead to higher overall profits.
   Again this is not the best method, demonstrating an ad hoc approach that leaves out assessment of opportunities in both the long and short term.

5. *Fixed sum per sales unit*: This method is similar to the percentage-of-sales approach, except that a specific amount per unit (e.g. per tonne sold) is used rather than a percentage of pound sales value. In this way, money for promotional purposes is not affected by changes in price. This takes an enlightened view that promotional expenditure is an investment, not merely a cost.

6. *What has been learned from previous years?*: The best predictor for next year's budget is this year's. Are results as predicted? What has been the relationship of spending to competition? What is happening in the market? What effect is it having and what effect is it likely to have in the future? It is important to:

   • experiment in a controlled area to see whether the firm is underspending or overspending
   • monitor results, by tracking the awareness of promotions amongst customers; this can be relatively easy, and the results of experiments with different budget levels can then be used in planning the next

step (although you must always bear in mind that all other things do not remain equal).

7. *Task method approach*: Recognising the weaknesses in other approaches, a more comprehensive four-step procedure is possible. Emphasis here is on the tasks involved in the process of constructing a promotional strategy as already described. The four steps of this method are as follows:

- *analysis*: make an analysis of the marketing situation to uncover the factual basis for promotional approach; marketing opportunities and specific marketing targets for strategic development should also be identified.
- *determine objectives*: from the analysis, set clear short- and long-term promotional objectives for continuity and build-up of promotional impact and effect.
- *identify promotional tasks*: determine the promotional activities required to achieve the marketing and promotional objectives
- *cost out promotional tasks identified*: what is the likely cost of each element in the communications mix and the cost-effectiveness of each element?

What media are likely to be chosen and what is the target (i.e. number of advertisements, leaflets, etc.)? For example, in advertising, the media schedule can easily be converted into an advertising budget by adding space or time costs to the cost of preparing advertising material. The promotional budget is usually determined by costing out the expenses of preparing and distributing promotional material, etc. Here a variety of options may need considering, balancing greater or lesser expenditure against larger or smaller returns.

The great advantage of this budgetary approach compared with others is that it is comprehensive, systematic and likely to be more realistic. However, other methods can still be used to provide 'ball-park' estimates, although such methods can produce disparate answers. For example:

- we can afford £10,000
- the task requires £15,000
- to match competition requires £17,500
- last year's spending was £8,500.

    Note:   the figures here may be on any scale, thousands, hundreds of thousands
    or more.

The decision then becomes a matter of judgement, making allowances for your overall philosophy and objectives. There is no widely accurate mathematical or automatic method of determining the promotional budget. The task method approach does, however, provide, if not the easiest, then probably the most accurate method of determining the promotional budget.

In a large company, or one with a substantial promotional budget, this will be carried out by, or with, an advertising agency, with certain of the tasks, such as media-buying or the creative input, being carried out exclusively by them. It is not necessary, nor is there the space here, to explore this planning process in detail, but it must be done, and done well. Even one simple (simple?) error can cause major problems. For example, you do occasionally see advertising for a new product on, say, television yet are unable to find it in the shops because the manufacturer has got the timing of advertising and stocking out of line. This can happen all too easily and cause problems, yet it can be very difficult for a company to control all the external factors exactly as it wishes. This kind of mistake can not only be costly, but alienate customer loyalty for the future.

# *Promotional planning*

**Introduction**

Because of the disparate nature of the various promotional techniques (see PROMOTION for an overview) it follows that selecting the 'right' mix and implementing the actual promotional activity is a complex task. So too is deciding how much to spend (see PROMOTIONAL BUDGET). Clearly success, in terms of promotion of any sort that works, does not 'just happen'; a systematic approach is necessary, and so is a degree of formality.

The following checklist presents a classic twelve-stage approach to the promotional planning process.

Essentially the approach described is designed to base promotion on an analysis of the market, putting together a plan of action that is most likely to relate accurately to the chosen objectives.

Of course, there is a rôle for creativity here – an important one as the sections on the individual techniques make clear. However, creativity must not be allowed to ride roughshod over other issues. Many a budget has been wasted because someone has had a creative idea and been given their head, yet results have been disappointing because the idea was implemented in a vacuum; without a clear focus on the purpose promotion will fail or at best be diluted.

## Checklist: Promotional planning

1. Analyse the market and clearly identify the exact need.
2. Ensure the need is real and not imaginary, and that support is necessary.
3. Establish that the proposed tactics are likely to be the most cost-effective.
4. Define clear and precise objectives.
5. Analyse the tactics available, taking into consideration the key factors regarding:

   • the market

- the target audience
- the product range offered
- the company organisation/resources.

6. Select the mix of tactics to be used.
7. Check the budget to ensure funds are available.
8. Prepare a written operation plan.
9. Discuss and agree the operation plan with all concerned and obtain management decision to proceed.
10. Communicate the details of the campaign to whoever is implementing it and ensure that they fully understand what they must do, and when.
11. Implement the campaign, ensuring continuous feedback of necessary information for monitoring performance.
12. Analyse the results, showing exactly what has happened, what factors affected the result (if any) and how much the campaign cost. (This stage may usefully include communication to all concerned to complete the circle.)

Nothing in the promotional plan must become automatic in the sense that a successful promotion is simply repeated without thought. Nothing lasts forever. Yet a promotion should not be ditched just because it is old. Many promotional tactics evolve, changing progressively to ensure they keep up to date with – or ahead of – their markets. Brand new ideas are needed as well.

Like so much else in marketing there is a balance to be struck. Creativity must assist promotional objectives to be met. If promotion becomes all wings and no feet, then however superficially clever the ideas, it will not work effectively. Again one might repeat the maxim that marketing is as much art as science; it is perhaps most true in the area of promotion.

So, to summarise here, promotion is something that encompasses a number of techniques. These need to be deployed against sound objectives, must be well co-ordinated and – perhaps above all – must be implemented creatively.

Though fashion and copying ('me-too' promotion) are evident in promotion, and particularly in advertising, originality and creativity are two very important aspects for any successful promotion. A creative and original scheme, even though inexpensive, can, and often does, score over a high-budget, stereotyped uncreative approach. While promotion can never sell a poor product (well, certainly not more than once), a well thought out and consistent approach can become memorable. Promotional and advertising slogans even pass into the language; at their best they can create an awareness of something, indeed a desire for it, which may be very difficult for a competitor to overthrow. Even if half the

money spent on promotion were wasted, the other half is very important.
Planning in this area is clearly worth the time and effort it takes; it creates a greater certainty of success.

**Definition:** *Prospecting*

This refers to the specific sales task of identifying and contacting new individual potential customers (prospects), which may be individuals or organisations; it is dealt with on page 152 within the section SALES FORCE AND SELLING.

# Public relations

**Introduction**

Public relations, often abbreviated to PR (careful: the same initials are used for Press Relations), is concerned, in a word, with image. Unless it is completely invisible, every organisation will have an image. But the question is whether it projects the right image, or sometimes whether there is a strategy to project anything at all.

Every organisation must ask itself what people think of it. In seeking to create (and then maintain and develop) an image, it helps to have, as a starting point, a clear idea of current customers' perception. This is something that can be researched through 'perception surveys'. But, of course, some information can be obtained just by 'keeping one's ear to the ground', although it is important to remember that people often say what they think is expected; or worse, what is heard only confirms the existing view, and perhaps existing prejudices.

The effect of public relations is cumulative and a host of factors, perhaps individually seeming of no major significance, are therefore important. These include the quality of business cards and letter-heads (indeed the whole graphic image), the quality of Switchboard and Reception, of all printed promotion, of staff appearance and service, and so on. A major influence also is exactly how people are dealt with: whether it is appropriate and corresponds with their image of good customer service. In this respect what one might call the 'image climate' is affected every time someone within the organisation has contact with a customer.

Consider any company which you know, one that has a strong image and of which you think well. Then think *why* this is so. Unless you have direct experience of them, it can only be because of what *they* tell you about themselves. Such messages can be powerful. Large companies will spend enormous amounts of money on their corporate image, something that hits the headlines occasionally (as with BT and British Airways recently, or the Pepsi Cola colour change which was implemented on a worldwide scale). But, large or small, the image matters. Everything from the overall logo (company symbol) in all its manifestations, to an individual's calling card.

Public relations must provide a planned, deliberate and sustained attempt to promote understanding between an organisation and its audiences. In fact, it must promote not just understanding, but a positive interest in the firm that whets appetites for more information, prompts enquiries, re-establishes dormant contacts and reinforces image with existing customers.

Not only is public relations activity potentially a powerful weapon in the promotional armoury, some aspects of it are also free – at least compared with advertising, which is communication in bought space. But there is a catch. It takes time! And, perhaps particularly in any small business, time is certainly money. Therefore, in too many organisations public relations is neglected because staff are busy, even over-stretched, and opportunities are missed. Yet if the power of public relations is consistently ignored, then at worst not only are opportunities missed but the image that is formed by default may actually damage business prospects.

In many ways, therefore, time spent on public relations is time well spent, and, while for smaller firms it can produce good low-cost results, a larger firm able to sub-contract the activity to a PR agency may well spend substantial sums to create a continuity of visibility in this way. If so, they will expect to see larger-scale results, and much of that comes potentially through the press. For more detail about what goes on in this area of marketing see PRESS RELATIONS.


## How you may be involved

Before you turn to that, however, it is worth ending this section by making the point that this area of marketing, almost by definition, involves many people throughout the organisation. Public relations links directly to a wide range of people in an organisation and to standards of service. Some well known fictitious examples can be seen in the award-winning training film *Who Killed the Sale?* (made by Rank – now Training Direct). The film shows a salesman trying, unsuccessfully, to get an order for some kind of engineering product (the product details do not matter). Progressively, we see the potential customer more and more unimpressed as he is exposed to others in the organisation and, cumulatively, such a poor image builds up that he is unwilling to place a new order – yet the salesman ends the film honestly wondering what went wrong.

A number of people and departments are involved:

1. The dispatch department, already at fault over a wrongly delivered order, makes matters worse by the incompetent way in which it attempts to sort out the problem.

2. The switchboard operator contributes to losing an important message for the customer, who is visiting the factory; so does a harassed girl in the sales office who fails to track him down.
3. A technician unconvincingly conducts a demonstration, failing to realise its importance because he, in turn, was poorly briefed.
4. Two other technical people are dismissive about the company's engineering competence, and their conversation is overheard by the customer.
5. The managing director lets internal matters, and hierarchy, override the service to the customer by demanding that the sales manager leaves the customer to attend an internal meeting; and the sales manager lets it happen.
6. And, the last straw, as the customer drives away from the factory he is held up, and made to reverse, by a rude delivery man; when the delivery man closes his van door, he reveals the name of the same potential supplying company.

Such a list, which spans the company from top to bottom, could be wider. Try thinking for a moment about your own company. What incidents can you remember? And can you list those people in a position to exert a positive influence on the process of building image – are you, perhaps, among them?

It takes few of these kinds of incident to negate all the time and money spent on an expensive corporate image.

---

**Warning**

If you have read any real amount of this book you will see that, almost regardless of your role in an organisation, you *are* involved. Failing to act on the basis of such an understanding is likely to dilute image or, at worst, cause real problems.

---

# Relationship marketing

**Introduction**

This term defines marketing that aims to build a relationship. Banks often promote themselves in this way: they are intent on creating and retaining a feeling of good – and individually directed – service, while ensuring that customers remain loyal and buy across the range (everything from traveller's cheques to mortgages, insurance and pensions).

The concept is that all aspects of marketing should be translated into something that reflects the individual nature of the relationship throughout. This is a difficult balance. Marketing, certainly from a bank, may be directed at many thousands of people, yet must try to keep an individual feel.

The various techniques used, for example telephone contact and direct mail (continuing to think of a bank) must sit comfortably alongside personal service – with 'comfortable' being defined by the customer.

Many companies use aspects of this approach, with varying degrees of success. Some make it very personal, creating a 'club' feel to the communication to try to make it seem more exclusive. Examples include major schemes such as frequent flyer programmes, loyalty schemes run by supermarkets and other chains, and more individual schemes run by much smaller companies.

**Definition:** *Retailing*

See DISTRIBUTION, and also MERCHANDISING for details of how marketing seeks to influence the in-store environment.

# Sales force and selling

### Introduction

There is an old saying that nothing happens until someone sells something, and in many businesses selling is indeed a vital part of the communications mix without it the rest of the promotional activity may be wasted.

Selling is the only persuasive technique which involves direct personal contact.

Selling can sometimes have an unfortunate image. Think of your own instant judgement on, say, a double-glazing or insurance salesman. The first words that may come to mind are 'pushy', 'high-pressure' or 'con-man'. Selling can be associated with pushing inappropriate goods on reluctant customers – selling refrigerators to Eskimos is perhaps the kind of situation which springs to mind in those not directly involved in sales (though Eskimos *do* buy refrigerators as they need them to keep food *warm* enough to cook without defrosting!).

The best – i.e. most effective – selling can be described as 'helping people to buy'. Much of it has advisory overtones and, if it is to be acceptable as well as effective, it cannot be pushy but must, like everything in marketing, be customer-orientated. Selling is, in fact, a skilled job and demands a professional approach from those who do it. Customers may want the product, but with plenty of alternative sources of supply they are demanding, and convincing them to do business with a particular supplier may be no easy task.

Perhaps the following light-hearted story (taken from my book *Everything You Need To Know About Marketing*, Kogan Page) makes the difficulty of the task clearer:

*Buyers are a tough lot*

It is any buyer's job to get the best possible deal for his company. That is what they are paid for: they are not actually on the salesmen's side, and will attempt to get the better of them in every way, especially on discounts.

This is well illustrated by the apocryphal story of the fairground strongman. During his act he took an orange, put it in the crook of his

151

arm and bending his arm squeezed the juice out. He then challenged the audience offering £10 to anyone able to squeeze out another drop.

After many had tried unsuccessfully, one apparently unlikely candidate came forward, he squeezed and squeezed and finally out came a couple more drops. The strongman was amazed, and, seeking to explain how this was possible, asked as he paid out the £10 what the man did for a living. "I am a buyer with Ford Motor Company*" he replied.

Buyers are not really like this; they are worse.

However, and wherever, selling must take place if the marketing process is to be successfully concluded. At one end of the scale it is simple. For example, an off licence may be able to increase sales significantly just by ensuring that every time a member of staff is asked for spirits, they ask, 'How many mixers do you want?' Many people will respond positively to what has been called the 'gin and tonic' effect: the linking of one product with another. Sometimes the question is even simpler: the waiter in a hotel or bar, for example, who asks 'Another drink?' is selling.

At the other end of the scale, sales do not come from the single isolated success of one interaction with the customer. A chain of events may be involved: several people, a long period of time and, importantly, a cumulative effect. In other words, each stage, perhaps involving some combination of meetings, proposals, presentations, and more meetings, must go well or you do not move on to the next.

So, bearing in mind that the detail of what is necessary will vary depending on circumstances, let us review both the stages and some of the principles involved, throughout the sales process.

Selling starts, logically enough, with identifying the right people to whom to sell. Sales time is expensive so it is important for sales people to spend time with genuine prospects, the more so when the longer lead time referred to above, and typical in the purchase of, say, computer systems, is involved. Some of the right people come forward as a result of promotional activity. They phone up, return a card from a mailshot, or whatever, and, in so doing, are saying, 'Tell me more'. Others have to be found; finding them is the first stage of the selling process.

## Locating prospects

This part of the process (which overlaps to some extent with marketing and promotion) is perhaps best described by way of a simple, everyday example.

---

* Whatever industry you are in you can doubtless think of customer names that would fit well here.

Consider a travel agent – someone in a business all managers probably deal with at some time or another. Its manager has a successful retail travel agency business. He identifies that, in addition to selling to customers over the counter, he is well placed to deal with commercial accounts in the area in which his business is located. He needs to initiate some contacts, but with whom? The first stage is to check. He looks at his files for companies he has dealt with previously and individual customers who work for the right kind of company. This produces some names but he needs more and considers a list of sources including:

- local Chambers of Commerce and Trade; not just by consulting their lists but perhaps by belonging to them or addressing their meetings
- public libraries: particularly as a source of some of the items mentioned later in this list
- his suppliers: among the companies he buys from, such as those who sell office equipment and supplies, some may be potential customers
- credit bureaux or other professional service agents
- personal observation: the factory down the road, the new office block on the corner
- local government offices
- referrals: existing customers, suppliers' customers, contacts or friends
- his bank
- mailing lists: often available for rent as well as from directories
- exhibitions and trade promotion events
- local hotels: who already receive business from him and may be helpful in return. What meetings or exhibitions go on there?
- company annual reports (from his public library)
- company house/employee magazines (from his public library)
- trade/industry/technical journals (from his public library)
- directories of companies (from his public library)
- telephone directories/yellow pages (from his public library).

One or a combination of these can supply valuable information about prospects: the names of companies, what business they are in, if it is going well or badly, whether they export, how big they are, who owns them, what subsidiaries or associates they have and, last, but certainly not least, who runs and manages them.

Exactly which individual is then approached is obviously vital, and may not be a simple decision. Indeed, it may be that more than one person is involved. For example, the person who travels, the person who sends him or her, the person who pays and perhaps also the person who makes the booking. There is many a secretary with considerable discretionary power in making company travel bookings, and not least among their considerations will be how straightforward and easy the travel agency is for them to deal with personally.

As well as considering which individual to approach, the other important assessment at this stage is that of financial potential. How much business might be obtained from them in, say, a year? This analysis will rule out some prospects as not being worth further pursuit. Experience will sharpen the accuracy with which these decisions can be made, but meantime a good first list is developing.

The old military maxim that 'time spent in reconnaissance is seldom wasted' is a good one. In war it can help to prevent casualties. In business it not only produces information, in this case about whom should be contacted, but also provides a platform for a more accurately conceived, and more successful, approach.

So having identified who will be contacted, his next step is organising the approach. A number of factors may be important here, both before an approach is made and in follow-up. Two key areas he needs to consider before making an approach are:

1. *How will the approach be made?* The ultimate objective is almost certainly a face-to-face meeting, which must be held before any substantial business can result. Such a meeting can be set up by:

   - 'cold calling', i.e. calling without an appointment
   - sending a letter or card with or without supporting literature
   - telephoning 'cold' or as follow-up to a letter or promotion
   - getting people together, initially as a group, and making a presentation at your premises, a hotel or other venue, or through a third party (such as at a Chamber of Commerce and Trade meeting).

   The logistics are also important. What is needed is a campaign spread over time so that if and when favourable responses occur they can be followed up promptly; such responses may be more difficult to cope with if they all occur together.

2. *Who will make the approach?* The process will almost certainly involve approaching, meeting and discussing matters with people senior in, and knowledgeable about, their own business. The approach therefore needs to be made by people with the right profile, who will be perceived as being appropriate, and who can really give an impression of competence. They will also need to have the right attitude, wanting to win business in what may be a new and perhaps more difficult area. And they need the knowledge and skills to tackle the task in hand: knowledge of the customers, the agency and its services, of overseas places and processes or the ability to discover these quickly.

Detail is important. The export manager who is made late for an appointment will be equally upset whether he has missed a flight connection or whether he has simply been misinformed on the time it takes to get from airport to hotel. The travel agent, rightly or wrongly, will probably get the blame. Finally, skills in customer contact, selling and negotiation are needed as well as skills in all other areas, such as writing sales letters, involved in making the approach. Making the right choice of person is therefore crucial, and in the long term, a small company set on developing its business travel side may need to consider recruitment, training or both.

The initial approach is vital, like any first impression, and it may be very difficult having received an initial negative response to organise a second chance. Having thought the process through in this way, the chances of success are that much greater.

However it is set up, once contact occurs, the sales person has to make and carry through a personal contact and to do this must understand the potential buyers and make his contact both persuasive yet acceptable; in other words not so 'pushy' as to be self-defeating.

## The sales process

Selling is an important element of marketing and it is worth reviewing in some detail just what it entails, so this is unashamedly the longest section of the book. It has been kept together so that the series of events constituting the sales process can be reviewed in sequence. Bearing in mind that many jobs involve a degree of persuasion, put yourself in a sales person's shoes and see how they must approach the task. You should find that some of the principles apply whenever an element of persuasion is necessary.

Selling starts, as detailed above, with an understanding of the buyer. No one can sell effectively without understanding how people make decisions to purchase. A good way of thinking about it, one originated by psychologists in America, suggests that the decision-making which goes on in the buyer's mind goes through seven, distinct, stages which may be paraphrased as follows:

1. I am important and I want to be respected.
2. Consider my needs.
3. How will your ideas help me?
4. What are the facts?
5. What are the snags?
6. What shall I do?
7. I approve.

Just think, for a second, what you do faced with a decision to purchase, say, a new refrigerator. You want to deal with someone who is not only polite but also concerned for the customer; indeed who is prepared to discover and take on board your needs (What size is necessary to fit the kitchen? What is your view of economy? Or price?). Someone whose suggestions helpfully bear in mind the brief, who gives you sufficient information on which to base a decision and who is able to handle your queries without becoming defensive or argumentative. And, not least, someone who explains – and makes clear and straightforward – any administrative points (delivery, payment terms, etc.), allowing you to make a decision confident that you will be pleased with your choice.

Any sales approach that responds unsatisfactorily to any of these stages is unlikely to end in an order. The buying mind has to be satisfied on each point before moving to the next, and to be successful a sales presentation sequence must match the buying sequence, and run parallel to it.

The two keys to success – or 'closing the sale' as obtaining a buying commitment is called – are the process of matching the buyer's progression through the decision-making process, and describing the product selectively, discussing it in a way that relates precisely to what a (particular) buyer needs.

Early on, because the customer needs to go through other stages, the sales person may not always be able to aim for a commitment to buy, but he must have in mind a clear objective on which to close. This may be to get the customer to allow him to send literature, to fix an appointment to meet or to provide sufficient information for a detailed quotation to be prepared. Whatever his objective is, however, it is important to know and be able to recognise the various stages ahead. With any customer contact (by telephone or letter as well as face to face), the sales person can identify:

- what stage has been reached in the buying process
- whether the selling sequence matches it and if not, why not
- what he needs to do if the sequence does not match
- whether a step has been missed
- whether he is going too fast
- if he should he go back in the sequence
- whether his objectives can still be achieved, or are they the wrong objectives
- how he can help the buyer through the rest of the buying process.

Naturally, the whole buying process is not always covered in only one contact between the company and the customer. Not every initial contact results in a sale; nor does it result in a lost sale. Some stages of the selling sequence have to be followed up in each sales contact, but the logic applies equally to a series of calls which form the whole sales approach to each customer. For a doubtful customer, or a sale of great complexity and expense, there may be numerous contacts to cover just one of the stages before the buyer is satisfied and both can move on to the next stage. Each call or contact has a selling sequence of its own in reaching the call objectives. Each call is part of an overall selling sequence aimed at reaching overall sales objectives.

Planning the selling sequence is therefore as much a part of call planning as it is of sales planning, but only rarely does a call take place exactly as planned. Knowing and using the sales sequence and being able to recognise stages of the buying process are, however, invaluable if sales people are to realise their potential for direct sales results.

With this basic appreciation of the buyer, and what is directing his or her reactions, we can look closer at the key areas of the sales approach.

## Using product information effectively

Identifying with the buyer, in order to recognise the stages of the buying process and to match them with a parallel selling sequence, must extend to the presentation of the sales proposition. Nowhere is this more important than in the way sales people look at the product, or service, which they are selling.

Product knowledge is too often taken for granted by companies and sales people. Sadly, experience of hearing hundreds of sales people talking unintelligible gibberish does not support this complacency. Sales people are too often given inadequate product knowledge and what is given is slanted towards the company, not the customer. Managers are often still heard to say proudly, 'Everyone joining us spends six months in the factory to learn the business', but many then emerge with no better idea of what the product means *to the customer*. Everyone with any role to play in sales-orientated customer contact must consider the product, and all that goes with it, from the customer's point of view.

## Selling benefits

If sales people get into the habit of seeing things through the customer's eyes, they will realise that they do not sell special promotions; free trial offers or fancy wrappings do not really sell products either. They sell what customers want to buy – not products or services themselves, but benefits.

But what are benefits? This concept is vital to successful selling and deserves a clear definition. Benefits are what products, promotions or services *do for* or *mean to* the customer. For example, a person does not buy an electric drill because he wants an electric drill, but because he wants to be able to make holes. He buys holes, not a drill. He buys the drill for what it will do (make holes). And this in turn may only be important to him because of a need for storage and a requirement to put up shelving.

When this is realised, selling becomes more effective and also easier. Sales people do not have to try to sell the same product to many different people, but meet each person's needs with personal benefits.

Benefits are what things sold can do for each individual customer – the things the customer wants them to do for him or her. Different customers buy the same product for different reasons. Therefore, you must identify and use the particular benefits of interest to them. It is important to remember two points:

1.  What a product *is* is represented by its features.
2.  What a product *does* is described by its benefits.

This is illustrated, showing also the relationship with the needs of customers, in Figure 11.

---

**Family car**
Need      Low cost – not expensive to run
Benefit   Good miles per gallon figures
Feature   Efficient engine design/fuel injection/aerodynamic profile

**A cooker**
Need      Must cope with the family
Benefit   Will grill six steaks at one time
Feature   A 200 square inch grill pan

**An accountant**
Need      Cost effective
Benefit   The right work with no disruption and at minimum cost
Feature   A computer assisted audit

**Venue for a wedding reception**
Need      Memorable
Benefit   Wedding photographs that people will love
Feature   An attractive eighteenth-century country house hotel
          with beautiful gardens

---

Note:  This approach also reduces the likelihood of using too much confusing jargon. For instance, digital circuitry may make a roving telephone more efficient, but that description is both a feature and jargon. Saying it is crystal clear and will work equally well in every room in a large house, because of the digital circuitry, starts with features, uses the feature to add credibility and is truly descriptive.

*Figure 11  Benefit and need examples*

If sales people forget this, then the things that are important to a customer will not always be seen as important from the seller's viewpoint, particularly if they have had little or no sales training. The result can, understandably, end up in a conflict of priorities, with the sales person concentrating on what is important to them (their company, product and the need to sell), while the customer unsurprisingly takes their own view, one that reflects their priorities and needs.

The customer is most unlikely to see things from the seller's point of view. Everyone is, to themselves, the most important person in the world. To be successful therefore, the seller has to be able to see things from the customer's point of view and demonstrate through their words and actions that he has done so. His chances of success are greater if he can understand the needs of the people he talks to and make them realise that he can help them to fulfil those needs.

To do this necessitates the correct use of benefits. In presenting any proposition to a customer, even simply recommending a product in reply to a query, sales people should always translate what they are offering into what it will do. Often, a company, and the people who write the sales literature, grow product-orientated, and gradual product development can reinforce this attitude by adding more and more features. It is only a small step before everyone is busy trying to sell the product on its features alone. It is interesting to note that often, when this happens, advertising and selling become more and more forceful, with the features being given a frantic push, as passing time reveals that there has been no great rush to buy.

Two examples, probably familiar to everyone, are the audio and camera markets. Stereo equipment, in particular, is almost always promoted on features only. Masses of technical terms, most of them meaningless to the majority of end-users, dominate advertisements and brochures, while the visual communication is based entirely on the appearance of the amplifier, speakers and other 'boxes'. Yet what people want from a stereo set is sound and reliability – years of listening pleasure. Cameras are often sold on the same, features-orientated, basis.

When competitive products become almost identical in their performance, it can be difficult to sell benefits, since all options seem to offer the same benefits. Choice then often depends on the personal appeal of some secondary feature. But even then, there must be emphasis on the benefits of those features, rather than on the features themselves. In industrial selling (to other companies rather than to individual consumers), it is more important than ever to concentrate on benefits rather than on features, which may be little better than gimmicks. Features are only important if they support benefits in which the customer is interested.

Deciding to concentrate on benefits is only half the battle, however. They have to be the right benefits. In fact, benefits are only important to a customer if they describe the satisfaction of his or her needs. Working out the needs, and then the benefits, means any sales person must put themselves in the customer's shoes.

## Who is the customer? What are their needs?

To know what benefits to put forward, the salesman must know what the customer's needs are. And to know them, he has to know exactly who the customer is. Very often, the customer is the user – the person who will actually use the product. But frequently, the direct customer is a purchaser or a decision-maker, not someone who is the user. This is most common in industrial selling, when a buying department is often responsible for ordering as well as handling the purchasing of most of a company's requirements. In consumer products, a manufacturer may sell to a wholesaler, the wholesaler to retailer, and it is only the retailer who actually sells to the users.

Naturally, the requirements of the end-user will also be of interest to the various intermediaries, but the best results will be obtained if sales people bear in mind the needs of both the buyer and the user, and the differences between their various needs.

Note that not all the needs will be objective ones. Most buyers, including industrial ones, also have subjective requirements bound up in their decisions. Figure 12 illustrates this concept, and shows that no product is bought on an entirely objective or subjective basis. Sometimes, even with technical products, the final decision can be heavily influenced by subjective factors, perhaps seemingly of minor significance, once all the objective needs have been met.

Matching benefits to individual customer needs makes a sale more likely, for a product's benefits must match a buyer's needs. The features are only what gives a product the right benefits.

By going through this process for particular products and for segments of the range, and by matching the factors identified to customer needs, a complete 'databank' of product information from the customer's viewpoint can be organised.

With competitive products becoming increasingly similar, more buyers quickly conclude that their main needs can be met by more than one product. Other needs then become more important. If, for instance, a buyer needs a crane, he is likely to find a number of them which will lift the weight required, and which will also cost practically the same. The deciding factors will then become availability, service and repair facilities, etc. A

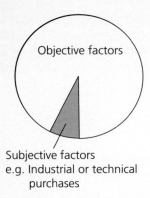
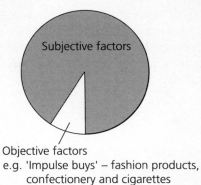

Subjective factors
e.g. Industrial or technical
purchases

Objective factors
e.g. 'Impulse buys' – fashion products,
confectionery and cigarettes

*Note: In fact most products/services are a more equal mix of the two extremes.*

*Figure 12 Subjective/objective reasons for buying using the benefit approach*

seller can look at the 'features' contained by the company as a whole and be ready to convert them to benefits to customers, in the same way as he can practise finding benefits for the full product range.

Every aspect of the company and its offering can, potentially, be described in terms of benefits. The table below illustrates this.

**Company features and customer benefits**

| Feature | Customer benefits | |
|---------|-------------------|---|
| Products | design<br>price<br>delivery<br>appearance<br>packaging | storage<br>workmanship<br>credit<br>stocks |
| Services | speed<br>availability<br>credit<br>after-sales service | training<br>advertising<br>merchandising<br>pre-sales advice |
| Companies | time established<br>reputation<br>location<br>philosophy | labour-relations<br>size<br>policies<br>financial standing |
| Staff | knowledge<br>skill<br>character | availability<br>training<br>specialists |

Each item listed above could be a source of benefit to potential customers, and as they recognise this they move closer to becoming actual customers. By 'thinking benefits' and by seeing things from the customer's point of view, sales people can make a real contribution to sales and company profitability.

## Jargon

A final hazard, which can destroy the customer-orientation of sales contacts, is jargon. This 'professional slang' comes in two main forms, both of which can confuse customers:

1. *Technical or industrial jargon*: Sales people should always let the customer be first to use this. Technological complexities have already led to thousands of new words and phrases in business and industry, and introducing still more new terms seldom helps. But worst of all is the possibility that the customer will not know what is being talked about, or will form the wrong impression, yet still hesitate to admit it.
2. *Organisation jargon*: It is even more important to avoid the internal jargon of a particular organisation, for here the customer will be on very unfamiliar ground. There is a world of difference between someone saying, 'We'll do a sales/stock return compo and let you know shortly' and, 'To answer your query, we'll have to do a comparison of the sales and stock return movements. The quickest way will be to ask for a computer printout which Head Office will forward to us. I will contact you with the answer in a week or ten days' time.'

Company jargon can have a wide effect, not only when used in selling, and even simple phrases can cause trouble. For example, delivery is one area for potential misunderstanding. Promising 'immediate delivery' might mean getting the product to the customer within a week, when normal delivery might take three weeks. But what if the customer is in the pharmaceutical industry, where 'immediate delivery' is jargon for 'within eight hours'? They are almost bound to get the wrong impression.

However, saying the right things is not all there is to selling: a critical stage is asking the right questions and listening – *really listening* – to the answers, using these as a guide to how to proceed.

## Asking the right questions in the right way

Knowing how and why customers buy is a pre-requisite to successful selling, and because all customers are individuals and want to be treated as such, so selling must be based on finding out exactly what each customer wants, and why. In other words, questioning (and listening to and using the answers) is as important to selling as is simply presenting the case.

It is important, therefore, to start asking questions early in the approach, and asking the right questions in the right way is crucial. Two characteristics are important in getting it right. They should be primarily:

1. *Open questions*: Those that cannot be answered by 'yes' or 'no', but get the customer talking. These work best and produce the most useful information.
2. *Probing questions*: Those that go beyond enquiring about the background situation, to explore problems and implications, and to identify real needs.

This approach can be illustrated by the following, hypothetical, conversation between the travel agent referred to above and one of his prospects:

*Agent*: What areas are currently your priority, Mr Export Manager?

*Prospect*: The Middle East is top priority for investigation but, short term, Germany has been more important.

*Agent*: What makes that so?

*Prospect*: Well, we're exhibiting at a trade fair in Germany. This will tie up a number of staff and eat up a lot of the budget. Our exploratory visit to the Middle East may have to wait.

*Agent*: Won't that cause problems, seeing as you had intended to go earlier?

*Prospect*: I suppose it will. With the lead times involved it may rule out the chances of tying up any deals for this financial year.

*Agent*: Had you thought of moving one of your people straight on from Germany to the Middle East, Mr Export Manager?

*Prospect*: Er, no.

*Agent*: I think I could show some real savings over making two separate trips. If you did it this way, the lead time wouldn't slip. Would that be of interest?

*Prospect*: Could be. If I give you some dates can we map something out to show exactly how it could be done?

*Agent*: Certainly . . .

This kind of questioning not only produces information but can be used creatively to spot opportunities. It accurately pin-points the prospect's real needs and allows an accurate response to them. Most prospects not only like talking about their own situation but react favourably to this approach. They may well see the genuine identification of their problems and the offer of solutions to them as distinctly different from any competitive approach they have received; such an approach may have simply catalogued the product or services offered.

In this case, it also clearly shows the two benefits that purchasers look for from travel agents: objectivity and expertise. The more these benefits are apparent, the more the agency is differentiated from the competition.

## The professional sales approach

So far this section has concentrated on certain factors inherent in the sales job, particularly those, like everything in marketing, which demand a customer-orientation and may be relevant to others in the company; these include finding out customer needs and talking benefits.

Of course, there is more to it than that, but a comprehensive analysis of selling is beyond the scope of this book. (The author's *101 Ways to Increase Sales*, Kogan Page, 1997, provides more detailed coverage of selling techniques).

A number of other factors, however, should be mentioned. First, the basics; to be successful, field sales staff must be able to:

1. *Plan*: They must see the right people, the right number of people, regularly if necessary.
2. *Prepare*: Sales contact needs thinking through; the 'born sales person' is very rare, the best of the rest do – and benefit from – their homework.
3. *Understand the customer*: Use empathy, have the ability to put themselves in the 'customer's shoes', to base what they do on real needs, to talk benefits.
4. *Project the appropriate manner*: Not every sales person is welcome, not everyone can easily position themselves as an advisor or as whatever makes their approach acceptable; being accepted needs working at.
5. *Run a good meeting*: Stay in control, direct the contact, yet make the customers think they are getting what they want.
6. *Listen*: A much undervalued skill in selling.
7. *Handle objections*: The pros and cons need debating; selling is not about winning arguments or scoring points.
8. *Be persistent*: Ask for a commitment, and, if necessary, ask again.

Secondly, a variety of additional skills may be necessary to operate professionally in a sales role. These include:

- account analysis and planning
- the writing skills necessary for proposal/quotation documents to be as persuasive as face-to-face contact
- skills of formal presentation
- numeracy and negotiation skills.

And all this in a job where people are sometimes referred to as being 'only in sales'.

Before moving on, two last factors which influences sales success deserve a mention:

1. *Sales management*: The sales manager, or whoever runs the sales team, is very much part of the marketing team and should have a direct influence over the degree of success achieved by their sales team (See SALES MANAGEMENT).
2. *Holding and developing customers*: There is an old saying that 'selling starts when the customer says yes', meaning that any company wanting long-term, repeat business, must work at it ensuring that the ongoing sales process continues to act to retain and develop business for the future.

The above principles can be illustrated by further reference to the travel agency manager. The manager knows that in winning more business travel the overall objective is not one order, but ongoing profitable business from this area. Whether customers are retained, buy again and buy more is dependent primarily on two factors:

1. *Service*: It almost goes without saying, but promises of service must be fulfilled to the letter; if they are not, the customer will notice. A number of different people may be involved in servicing the account. They all have to appreciate the importance of getting their part right.

    If the customer was promised information by 3.30pm, a visa by the end of the week, two suggested itineraries in writing and a reservation in a certain hotel at a particular price, then the customer should get just that. Even minor variations, such as information by 4pm and a slight price difference on room rate, do matter. Promise what can be done. And do it 100 per cent.
2. *Follow-up*: Even if the service received is first class, the customer must continue to be sold to after the order as follows:

    - Check with them after their trip.
    - Check who else is involved in the next purchase. Their secretary? Other managers?

- Ask more questions. When is their next trip? When should they be contacted again?
- Make suggestions. Can they book earlier? Would they like to take their spouse on their next trip?
- Anticipate. Do they know fares are going up? Can they make the trip earlier and save money?
- Explore what else they might buy.
- Investigate who else in the company travels. Other staff, departments, subsidiaries?
- See whether you can distribute holiday information among the staff
- Write to them, do not let them forget you. Make sure they think of you first.

A positive follow-up programme of this sort can maximise the chances of repeat business and ensure that opportunities to sell additional products or services are not missed.

Such an approach brings us full circle, from identifying and contacting prospects for the first time, to holding and developing their business on a continuing basis.

> *Note:  The techniques of selling are, simply put, those of persuasive communication. As such they can be useful in many circumstances; for more about this see* INTERNAL SELLING.

---

**Warning**

Selling is sometimes regarded as an unimportant part of marketing (something this section has been at pains to contradict). If this is the case in an organisation, it is a big mistake. Sales really is the final link with the customer, and if it is not working well the company is losing business. Selling is as much a strategic element of marketing as any other.

---

# Sales management

**Introduction**

Closely linked to the topic of the sales process and the sales team who are involved in it (see SALES FORCE AND SELLING), it is necessary to make brief comment about sales management. It is not enough for a company simply to push sales people out into the field and say: 'Sell'. Much as anyone else, sales people need managing – why else have a sales manager? – as do most organisations of any size. Usually a sales manager is very much part of the overall management and marketing team. In a small company they may have many tasks and responsibilities that are really general management functions.

The sales manager often handles a certain number of customers, usually larger ones, personally. There is nothing wrong with this, indeed such involvement is useful, but it can dilute the time available for the classic sales management functions and this, in turn, can leave sales less effective. Certainly it seems that in industries which put suitable time into managing a sales team, the investment it represents is regarded as both necessary and worthwhile. Normally the classic tasks of sales management are seen as falling into six areas, which reflect the need to:

1. *Plan*: Time needs to be spent planning the scope and extent of the sales operation, its budget and what it will aim to achieve. Achievement is organised first around targets – and setting targets – not just for the amount to be sold, but for profitability, product mix, etc. If the product range is large then this makes it especially important that the team's activities are directed with the right focus.

2. *Organise*: How many sales people are required needs calculating (not just a matter of what can be afforded, but of customer service and coverage; though the two go together), as does how and where they are deployed. The question of the various market sectors involved must also be addressed, looking at not just who calls on customers in, say, Hertfordshire, but how major accounts are dealt with and the strategy for any non-traditional outlets which may well need separate consideration. Organisations who sell to groups of customers that differ

167

radically from each other may separate the different sales tasks, and even have separate sales teams.

3. *Staff*: This is vital: it is no good, as they say, 'paying peanuts and employing monkeys'. If the sales resource is going to be effective then it must be recognised that recruitment and selection need a professional approach and the best possible team must be appointed. The job is to represent the firm, to differentiate from competition and sell effectively – certainly and continuously. Recruitment may be a chore, but selecting the best of a poor bunch (rather than re-advertising and starting the whole thing over again) should simply not be an option. It is also evident from even a cursory scan of typical job advertisements how much emphasis, in many industries, is put on past experience. As people tend to be sought at a youngish stage (when they are cheaper?) it might be an idea to consider new blood. The experience route is fine, but one effect can be to encourage poor performers to circulate around a particular industry; and if someone only did an average job for one company, what makes it likely that they will suddenly do better for another?

4. *Train*: As the process is ongoing, perhaps 'develop' is a better word here. Because there is no one 'right' way to sell, it is necessary to use appropriate approaches day by day, meeting by meeting, customer by customer, and continue to fine-tune both the approaches and the skills that generate them over the long term. If the team is to be professional in this sense, then more than a brief induction is necessary: ongoing field development is necessary.

It is simply not possible to run a truly effective team without spending sufficient time with individuals in the field, using accompanied calls first to observe and evaluate, and then to counsel and fine-tune performance. Without this, performance can never be maximised, indeed a whole area of activity is going by default. Although results show what is being achieved, figures alone cannot, by definition, show *how* things are being done in the field and whether performance could benefit from fine tuning. Only by direct involvement can sales management put themselves in a position to know what action might improve performance, and take it. Many would regard this as certainly the single most important aspect of the sales management job. The reason is entirely practical – time spent on it acts to increase sales. Not least, the process is valuable is ensuring that sales people adopt a practical and constructive approach to what they can do day-to-day to refine their own techniques and improve performance. Whatever the support given by sales management, the sales people themselves are, after all, the only coach there all the time.

5.  *Motivate*: Like development, motivation does not just happen (this is true of so much in management), it needs time, effort and consideration. Sales people, by definition, spend a great deal of time on their own – and can be exposed to negative attitudes from customers who are not exactly 'on their side' – and as a group need considerable motivation. Like training, motivation is not simply a 'good thing': it increases sales and makes performance more certain. Again sales management must work at this area systematically. It affects overall issues such as pay and other rewards (e.g. any commission scheme must act as a real *incentive* – not simply reward past performance – and thus must be well conceived and arranged). Motivation also affects many smaller issues. Just saying 'well done' helps motivation and how many managers, whatever their rôle, can put a hand on their heart and swear they have found time to do even that sufficiently often in, say, the last month? There is so much involved here – communications, effective sales meetings and good organisation. For example, letting a sales person act without good support material to show may well make selling more difficult and thus be demotivating. This is doubly so if those struggling to sell feel that inefficiency somewhere in the organisation is the cause of the problem. So motivation has a broad remit and involves a wider group of people than the sales manager alone.

6.  *Control*: Constant monitoring is necessary if the team is to remain on track and thus hit targets. Action must be taken to anticipate and correct any shortfall and this is traditionally the role of control. It is at least as important, however, to monitor *positive* variances. If something is going better than plan, then the reasons need to be identified – maybe there are lessons to be learned that can help repeat the good performance or spread the effect more widely.

All in all, sales management has a wide and vital brief. Figure 13 shows the various tasks as a continuum, highlighting the longer- and shorter-term aspects of the job. The chart was developed by my partner in Touchstone Training & Consultancy, David Senton.

The quality of sales management is often readily discernible from the state of the sales team. Excellence in sales management makes a real difference. Time spent on all aspects of sales management can have direct influence on sales results. The full detail of what is involved is beyond the scope of this work. There are whole books on sales management and for some it may be an area worth further study.

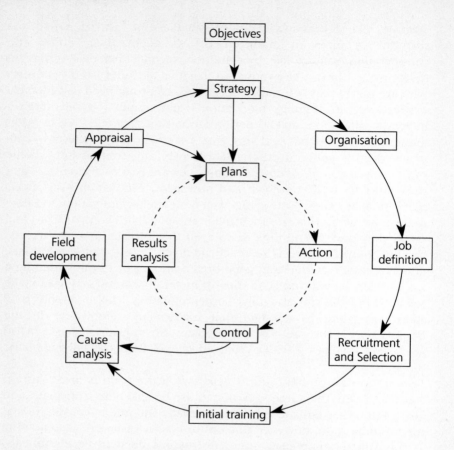

*Figure 13  Sales management long-/short-term tasks and responsibilities*

# Sales productivity

**Introduction**

The word 'selling' instantly conjures up the thought of the face-to-face encounters that form the bulk of sales work. And, of course, these have to be effective; but other elements are important also. So, the concept of *sales* productivity is certainly as valid as productivity is in any more traditional context. We might describe it as the sales equivalent of working smarter rather than just harder.

Whatever quality is brought to sales calls, sales results are influenced by more than this. The other crucial factors are:

- who is seen (the selection of appropriate prospects/buyers/customers)
- how many people are seen
- how often they are seen (the call frequency decided upon and how it varies and is used).

If these productivity factors are well organised and worked at on a regular basis then the overall results are likely to be improved; it is a differentiating factor between the good and less good sales people in any industry, and applies, albeit in slightly different ways, to all categories of customer, depending on the nature of the business.

Productivity comes first from seeing the right people, and the right outlets; and also the right individuals throughout larger outlets where sales people may have to see several people in different departments (as in selling, say, training to a company where purchase might be made by Personnel, Training or functional departments).

Secondly, it comes from sheer quantity. As long as call quality is not sacrificed, then the more people are seen the more will be sold. And third, there is the question of frequency. The oft-cited rule here is to call the *minimum* number of times that will preserve and build the business. Some accounts are called on every week. Others may be seen only once a year. Anyone, and this may affect smaller companies especially, must consider frequency very carefully. Sometimes purely personal factors influence this sort of productivity. On a wet Friday afternoon in an English February the author was tempted to go for a convenient call mid-afternoon – one which was en route for home where a reasonable welcome and a nice cup of tea were likely! – rather than to maximise productivity.

What is the frequency that will create some sort of continuity, how quickly do memories fade, what about the industry cycle, buying cycle, seasonality or financial year? Many factors may need to be considered in making a judgement. These factors and more are all important – as are the economics involved – but customer service is always important and if frequency falls below a certain level, any real continuity becomes difficult if not impossible to create.

This is an area for considered action, not an unthinking reiteration of the existing pattern. The detail here makes a difference and it is worth some time in analysis, planning and fine tuning to get it right.

# Sales promotion

## Introduction

Promotion is an umbrella term (see PROMOTION). Sales promotion, defined here in formal marketing terms, is 'an inducement aimed directly at persuading a specified target audience to achieve one or more defined objectives'; in simpler terms, it is a method of persuading people to take a course of action which, without that persuasion, they would not otherwise take. It encompasses or links to areas such as point of sale (POS), offers, giveaways, and merchandising and display in retail situations.

Sales promotion is an aid to selling, not a substitute for it. It is the tactic that is used because, after careful analysis of the facts and quantification of the objectives, it is likely to prove the most *cost-effective* method of meeting those objectives.

Sales promotion is not the answer if:

- all else looks doomed to failure
- the sales force has a period of inactivity
- someone thinks it would be nice to have some
- someone thinks they have a good idea.

Yet, perhaps because it is an 'ideas' area, this is precisely what can sometimes happen. If the company tries to make a problem fit an idea, instead of creating a planned scheme to solve the problem, then experience shows that there is a very great chance that it will not work. Remember that, as with any area of promotion, if it is not precisely *planned* and *controlled*, it could well have the directly opposite effect from the one it sets out to achieve.

## The rôle of sales promotion in marketing

Sales promotion is not an incidental that should only be used as an afterthought; nor should it be left to area sales staff to plan and implement.

It is an integral part of the marketing mix and, as such, requires the same degree of planning as does the mounting of a market-research project, or the selling-in of a new product. Effective planning is, therefore, essential, whether sales promotion is to be used as a support activity for the company's long-range objectives or as a short-term tactic.

A more specific way of understanding what sales promotion can do for the company is to summarise some of the major purposes of sales promotion, or the objectives that can be achieved through using it effectively in various ways. These are:

1. To introduce new products, by motivating customers to try a new product or retail customers to accept it for resale.
2. To attract new customers, by motivating people to try a new product or retail customers to accept it for resale for the first time.
3. To maintain competitiveness, by providing preferential discounts or special low prices to enable more competitive resale prices to be offered.
4. To increase sales in off-peak seasons, by encouraging consumption 'out of season'.
5. To increase trade stocks, by special monetary discounts or quantity purchasing allowances, in return for holding greater than normal levels of stock.
6. To induce present customers to buy more, e.g. by competitions to encourage them to think of more ways and more occasions for using the product.

Such a list cannot be definitive; there are many options and many circumstances where sales promotion can contribute. Generally, then, sales promotion is a marketing device to stimulate or re-stimulate demand for a product during a particular period. It cannot overcome deficiencies in a product's style, quality, packaging, design or function, but can provide an important addition to advertising activities as an integral part of the communications mix.

## Types of promotion

We will now turn to some examples of what can be done. This list, too, is unlikely to be comprehensive as a new promotional idea is thought up somewhere every minute of the day. Indeed, there are no hard and fast rules for selecting the 'right' sales promotion tactic, since what is successful in achieving an objective in one situation may not necessarily be successful in achieving a similar objective in another. Equally, the same promotion tactic might be suitable for meeting different objectives.

In practice, there are likely to be many alternatives, all of which would be suitable for meeting the same objective. Selection can be made easier by answering the following questions:

- Which promotion tactic best fits the profiles of the target audience?
- What are the advantages of each promotion tactic?
- What are the disadvantages of each promotion tactic?
- Which is likely to give the greatest level of success for the budget available?
- Which promotion best lends itself to accurate measurement of its effectiveness?

The types of promotion tactic currently available are many and, while they cannot be strictly confined to set categories, the following list shows something of the range:

1. *Promotions received at home*: In-home consumer promotions can help to pre-empt the attempts of competitors to solicit impulse purchases via in-store advertising and display. Techniques used here include:

   - sampling, where a sample of the product is delivered free to consumers' homes; clearly this has to be something suitable for home delivery (e.g. a tea bag) for this to work
   - coupon/voucher offers via postal and door-to-door distribution, newspaper or magazine distribution, and in-pack/on-pack distribution
   - competitions.

2. *In-store promotions*: Not all products are purchased in retailers, of course, but clearly, this type of promotion has the major advantage of featuring at the location where many of the *final* decisions and actual purchases for many products are made. Techniques used here include:

   - temporary price reductions
   - extra-value offers, including offers relating to future purchase (e.g. the major supermarkets' various Privilege card schemes)
   - premium offers (incentives), including free mail-in premiums, self-liquidating premiums and banded free gifts (e.g. free conditioner with a bottle of shampoo)
   - point-of-sale product demonstrations
   - personality promotions.

3. *Immediate benefit promotions*: Here, consumer reward for purchasing is immediate and, as with most incentives, the sooner the reward can be expected and received after the qualifying action, the greater will be the positive effects of that incentive in stimulating purchase action. Included in this promotion category are:

- price reductions
- free gifts (which can be additional product – two for the price of one; enabling greater value to be given at lower cost)
- banded pack offers (mentioned above)
- economy (special editions and own brand such as a Ryman's diary compared with the branded equivalent).

Some of these are offered by retailers as part of other broader schemes. For example, you can currently obtain Shell Smartcard points (or Airmiles) at John Menzies outlets which sell a range of stationery and other products.

4.  *Trade promotions*: Some promotions are directed exclusively at retailers or their staff. The reasons for promoting to the trade include:

    - obtain support and co-operation in stocking and promoting products to customers
    - to induce distributors to increase their stock levels, where research may have revealed lower-than-average stockholding
    - to pre-empt competitive selling activities by increasing trade stocks.

Amongst the techniques used in trade promotion are:

- *Bonusing*, which can take the form of monetary discounts or 'free goods' (13 products for the price of 12), or special quantity rate terms
- *Incentive schemes*, which can be tailored to the needs of a retailer's sales staff and may also include competitions, particularly for sales staff, e.g. competitions linked to generating window displays, with prizes such as holidays regularly used
- *Dealer loaders*, where instead of money, gift incentives may be offered to distributors, or their sales force, for achieving agreed sales targets or stocking certain quantities of product.

Clearly, trade promotion can be an extremely important element within the total market strategy in helping to ensure that stocks are available in the right distribution channels and at the right time.

Other techniques are:

- *Co-operative advertising schemes*, where a manufacturer gives assistance with preparation of advertisements or media costs, paying all or part of the cost of some promotion (one manifestation of this is the many small shops that incorporate a supplier's name in the sign over the shop)
- *Provision of display materials*, either free of charge or on a shared-cost basis (these can range from a display stand to a refrigerator)
- *Tailor-made promotions*, custom designed to the outlet's individual

requirements and often promoting their own name and corporate image.

While sales promotion was pioneered in the area of FMCG products (Fast Moving Consumer Goods) where it is most visible, it is also used, albeit in slightly different ways, to influence any kind of retailer, wholesalers and others, such as distributors. Its use can be very specific; reasons might include the need to:

- encourage repeat purchase and build loyalty
- secure marginal buyers
- meet competitive offers
- ensure that bills are paid on time (or sooner!)
- motivate the retailer's sales assistants
- induce rapid market penetration when launching something new
- sustain perception of value over and above that intrinsically possessed by the product itself
- smooth out costly buying cycles and seasonality.

If behaviour can be changed in these ways, to whatever extent, then a company will be more productive and profitable. Promotions are not always effective, but when they are they may have a considerable effect; and to achieve that they need to work rather than be unique.

Other aspects of the process need to be got right. Administratively, things must work well and be efficient. If a gift is included it must be of reasonable quality: complaints take a while to sort out and lose goodwill. Who does not still remember the fiasco of the Hoover promotion using flights to the United States? The difficulties and complaints resulting from this promotion did more harm than good.

A good promotion is usually transient (soon having to be replaced by something else) but can focus attention, boost sales and contribute to longer-term objectives as well. It is a positive way to build business, with the proviso, as with so much in promotion generally, that it must be appropriate to product, customers and circumstances. A tacky ballpoint pen is unlikely to boost sales of, say, a high-quality range of china, however many are given away with a dinner service.

**Definition:** *Segmentation*

See MARKET SEGMENTS.

**Definition:** *Selling*

See SALES FORCE AND SELLING.

**Definition:** *Social marketing*

The term social marketing refers to marketing activity carried out by non-profit-making organisations; or rather by those organisations or bodies which *intentionally* do not aim to make a profit! These may include government departments (e.g. in their promotion intended to reduce drink-driving), and campaigning and fund-raising bodies. They may use a whole range of marketing techniques, and many do so on a basis at least as sophisticated as that of their commercial cousins.

The term is primarily associated with those organisations, such as charities, who have some worthwhile purpose.

# Sponsorship

**Introduction**

Sponsorship is simply a specialised form of advertising. It works by associating the product with some other area of activity. Many examples come from the world of sport, with whole sports or individual events linked to commercial companies. In this kind of area most companies involved will be large, often FMCG, and with substantial budgets as costs can be high.

Another area where sponsorship is prevalent is in the arts. Programmes in theatres and concert halls bear witness to the fact and a great range of companies make use of it, including business-to-business marketing companies. Sponsorship links to corporate entertaining. Companies do not just sponsor an event, they make use of it by taking customers or distributors to events and laying things on to impress them. The scale may be wide and global (e.g. the sponsoring of an international tournament by a multi-national company) or small and local (e.g. sponsoring an event in one town).

There are dangers to this approach. Some companies may owe their decision to sponsor something less to objective thinking than to their chairman's fanatical love of, say, athletics. In addition, it can be hard to impress a client in the midst of a performance of *Madame Butterfly*; some events lend themselves more to conversation than others. Despite these reservations sponsorship can work well and is responsible for putting very large sums of money into areas that might wither without it.

**Definition:** *Surveys*

This is a term applied to certain types of research. Literally, a survey surveys; the term is imprecise and used for a variety of research activities, but particularly for those that review on a broad front or on a regular basis.

There is, for example, a survey of television audience viewing figures (how many people watch which channels at what times and for how long) which is conducted regularly. The document describing the findings is likely to be referred to as a survey. Conversely, a manufacturer checking on some detailed market factor is more likely to commission research which will set out findings in a report.

# *SWOTs*

**Introduction**

SWOTs is an acronym of: Strengths, Weaknesses, Opportunities and Threats. It acts as a basis for analysis of current and future situations inside (S and W) and outside (O and T) the organisation; this analysis is vital to marketing planning. (See MARKETING PLANNING.)

The sort of questions that are used during an analysis illustrate SWOTs more fully. The analysis below was conducted by a publisher.

## An organisation's strengths and weaknesses

1. *Customer base*

   - What is our current customer base, by size, by location, by category?
   - How does our disposition of customers (customer mix) compare with the market mix?
   - Are our customers in growth sectors of the market?
   - How dependent (as a specific measurement) are we on our largest customers?

2. *Range of services*

   - How closely does our product range reflect the market's needs?
   - How does our range compare with those of our competitors?
   - Are the majority of our areas of business in growth or decline?
   - Is the span of our product range too narrow to satisfy our markets?
   - Is our product range too broad to allow satisfactory management of performance across the range?

3. *Price structure*

   - What is the basis of our pricing policy?
   - Do our direct and indirect competitors structure in the same way?
   - Are our prices competitive?
   - Do our customers perceive our prices as offering 'value for money'?

4. *Promotional and selling activities*

- With which customer groups are we communicating?
- What do they know and feel about us?
- Are we communicating with enough of the 'right' people (both groups and individuals)?
- What means of communication are we using?
- What attitudes exist internally that influence approaches to promotion and selling?
- Is each person in contact with customers capable of selling the full breadth of our range, and doing so equally well for every element of it?
- Do they possess the necessary knowledge and skill for selling?

5. *Planning marketing activity*

- Do we have agreed plans for marketing and selling?
- Do the plans state specific activities as well as objectives and budgets? Are they measurable and monitorable?
- Do we have individual/departmental as well as corporate plans?

6. *Organising for marketing*

- How is the firm's marketing activity organised and co-ordinated?
- Are authority and responsibility for each person/activity clearly defined?
- Are all our people committed to contributing to a marketing culture that will assist the achievement of commercial success?

7. *Control and measurement of marketing*

- Have we defined 'success' for ourselves and our staff?
- Have we established all the necessary key result areas to measure that success?
- Do these standards examine marketing as well as publishing goals and standards?
- Do we measure performance against desired standards and take appropriate (and prompt) corrective action?

## Market opportunities and threats

1. *How is the market structured quantitatively?*

- How many people/organisations of what type are there in our market who need our kind of product?
- What are their current buying practices?

- How much do they spend on such items?
- How often do they buy (e.g. annually/monthly)?
- Who do they buy from currently?
- What do they not buy?
- How do existing and potential buyers access our market and our kinds of products?

2.  *How is the market structured qualitatively?*

    - Why do existing and potential customers buy/not buy?
    - What do they think of what they buy (e.g. good value/overpriced, etc.)?
    - What do they think of those who supply their current needs (e.g. too big/too small/helpful/unhelpful)?

3.  *How is the market served competitively?*

    - Who are our direct competitors (i.e. other similar firms)?
    - Who are our indirect competitors (i.e. 'overlapping' firms, some of which it may be easy to overlook as uncompetitive)?
    - What are their strengths and weaknesses (e.g. list size/staff/image / pricing/marketing skills/geographical coverage, etc.)?

4.  *What are the quantitative and qualitative trends?*

    - market/segment size
    - market/segment requirements
    - market/segment structure
    - market/segment location
    - competition.

Such an analysis is an invaluable tool in charting a course into the future. Which areas are most important will vary depending on the size and type of organisation concerned. It may seem a daunting task, and indeed it is a significant one, but once it has been addressed then it only needs updating and carrying forward; it is not necessary to start again with a blank sheet of paper. This is part of what is called a 'rolling' plan: one that builds on the past as it moves on to the next year and beyond.

## A practical way forward

The questions in the example above form a starting point. Certainly they are indicative of the sort of thinking that must be done, and of the sort of information which needs to be gathered before effective operation can follow. Every company needs to tailor its approach to this kind of thinking, both in terms of the nature of the company and the nature of the markets in which it operates. Customers will be defined very differently, for example, if an organisation sells direct or sells only to, say, the computer industry, when the power of the retail chains may not be of concern. It is important that all the specifics of your particular mode of operation are accommodated.

# Telemarketing

## Introduction

This is a term used to describe marketing where the main means of communication is the telephone, from initial contact right through to the delivery of the product or service.

Insurance, for example, is now often organised on this basis. The customer telephones for a quote (often using a free or local rate number, though the staff may be anywhere in the country, or even abroad, rather than at one central office) and everything thereafter is dealt with by telephone. Telephone banking is another example; this is very successful and has massive investment in service centres.

Products can also be sold this way, with dispatch following the telephone conversation. The amount done on the telephone and how it links to other factors may vary (another imprecise term) but its use is justified by the way marketing views the telephone as a main aspect of marketing.

> *Note:* *Telemarketing is not the same as telephone selling or telesales which implies only the sales part of the marketing activity is geared to the telephone, as in large-scale applications such as the sales of classified advertisements. This area overlaps with what sales people do either in keeping in touch to prompt repeat orders or in prospecting – 'cold calling' – to make first contact, often followed by arranging an appointment to meet.*

See also SALES FORCE AND SELLING and TELESELLING.

# *Teleselling*

**Introduction**

This term, which links with telemarketing (see TELEMARKETING), is used for a range of types of selling where the individual contacts are made by telephone.

Such contacts include:

- individual sales people making initial contact to seek an appointment
- sales people contacting customers on an agreed basis to obtain repeat orders; this works well where the customer needs to reorder on a regular basis to replace stock, e.g. a printer ordering paper
- substantial sales operations where little or no contact other than that on the telephone takes place; e.g. the sale of classified advertisements in a newspaper.

There is an overlap here, with the terms teleselling and telemarketing sometimes being alternated.

**Warning**

This is an area of marketing that has a bad image. It works well in many circumstances, but rubs people up the wrong way in as many others. It therefore needs undertaking, in terms of both its set-up and systems and its manner, with great care. The first job of selling on the telephone is to persuade people it is a natural and useful way for them to buy.

Upsetting customers creates negative images; and gets talked about.

**Definition:** *Test marketing*

This is the process of undertaking a launch of a new product on a limited basis, often in a small geographical area, to reduce risk.

See more details within the section: NEW PRODUCT LAUNCH.

## Introduction

More marketing jargon: the letters stand for Unique Selling Proposition. The idea is that every product or service should be analysed to see what gives it a special appeal in the market place. If there is not a USP, one may have to be created.

Marketing is sufficiently complex these days that the idea has been rather overtaken by events. To be successful a product needs to have a number of appeals in the market, to be value for money and get a host of details ranging from its price to its name right. Right can be defined only as meaning creating success.

A single USP in the sense of some 'magic formula' is unlikely to carry the day.

**Definition:** *Value-added marketing*

See ADDED VALUE.

# *Window display*

**Introduction**

This is a key part of the task retail marketing has of getting potential customers into any kind of shop.

All sorts of factors contribute to this – image, location, parking, etc. – but one factor of obvious importance is the impact made by the shop front, particularly the window and any window display in it (there is not always a display, as some windows are used exclusively to give a view of the shop interior, but the intention is the same).

Different approaches are used: some windows are busy and full of many different products; others have some more dramatic display, in some cases not linked directly to products at all (witness the Christmas displays in many department stores which are simply — or, not so simply usually – decorative).

In technique terms this would normally be regarded as part of the overall area of shop layout; see DISPLAY AND MERCHANDISING for more details about this overall marketing technique.

# Z chart

**Introduction**

The last heading: this is a bit of a cheat, but it is neat to have an A–Z book ending with a Z.

Seriously, however, the inclusion of Z charts does allow a comment to be made about control. The management control of activities and results is a key part of the activity of any marketing manager. This is for two reasons. First, targets are not just a cosmetic part of the management process, there can be a great deal hanging on them (if products are not sold as predicted, then the warehouse overflows; if they sell more quickly than planned, then supply may be a problem and customers get upset at delays).

Control monitors performance and allows action to be taken to fine-tune what is happening. Sometimes this is to close a gap, to increase performance and remove a shortfall in performance; on other occasions it is to analyse success, seek the reasons for it (especially if it is of an unexpected level or type) and then try to build on it for the future.

Good control and fine-tuning mean more successful marketing. In an uncertain and competitive world nothing else will do.

And the Z chart? This allows review of certain key indicators on one graph which sets out the picture succinctly, making it easier to take action. The name, unsurprisingly, comes from the shape.

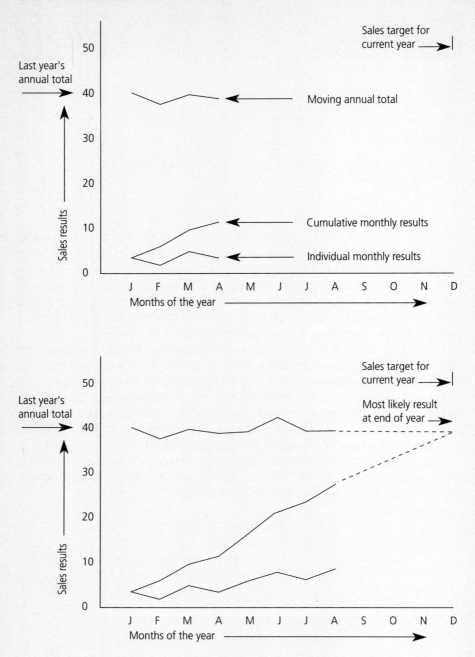

*Figure 14  The development of a Z chart.*

# Afterword

Whatever your interest in marketing, and wherever you sit in your organisation in relationship to it, you should, having read this far, have a better understanding of it, in concept and in its activities. Because it is very much more than a euphemism for sales or advertising you should also have a clearer idea as to how it impinges on your own business rôle. One overview factor dealt with was the marketing mix – what are sometimes called the three 'P's (four if you include 'place'). Even good products do not sell themselves and, while product quality is paramount, it is clearly no panacea and much else influences the degree of success any particular product will enjoy; marketing is nothing if not wide and fundamental in its influence.

To summarise and round off this review, perhaps I can end with what I call the five 'C's.

The first C is *customer*. The whole essence of every aspect of marketing – the concept, the planning through to all the research, communications and the application of every technique – must focus on the customer. The customer is king, as the saying has it: the customer is ultimately also the piper who calls the tune. This is something that is true of any business. Knowledge of and respect for the customer, however that word is defined and however many categories of customer there may be, is essential to business success. Some customers are disproportionately powerful (e.g. Tesco in the food business) and all may be fickle, with behaviour that is difficult to predict. Success, in part, goes to those who keep the closest eye on their customers.

The second C is *continuous*. Marketing is not an option, a bolt-on activity, or for moments when 'time allows'; it must be present all the time as a company goes about its business. Indeed, without marketing, there is a good chance it will *not* go about its business, at least for long. This also means that planning is crucial or marketing will always be *ad hoc*. Marketing must command support within the organisation if it is to receive the budget its work demands, and it must command the co-operation of others throughout the company who must work alongside it, if a strong and effective programme of marketing activity is to be successfully implemented. Monitoring marketing activity through research similarly deserves to be regular rather than only undertaken as a 'one-off' approach.

The next C is *co-ordinated*. Unless the many and various techniques of marketing are made to act together their effectiveness will be diluted. The different factors, sales and advertising, say, are not alternatives; all are necessary. When, how and how much all the techniques interrelate and overlap is down to the skill of those involved. Often this ongoing need for co-ordination is made more difficult by the number of people involved. This is especially true in a large organisation, but many may have people spread across many departments and, sometimes, spread geographically – maybe even across the world. Marketing is, in the true sense, a management function and, as was made clear in the introduction, must stem from a senior level.

The fourth C is *creativity*. Above, all marketing must differentiate and, in what seem to be ever more competitive times for most, to do so is a challenging task – more so in any business that neglects marketing or has done in the past. It is this combination of competitiveness and creativity which makes marketing so dynamic. It is not an exact science, and many of the variables that affect it are external. One never knows, for instance, what competitors will do next. So, however the necessary creativity shows itself – through product innovation, clever (or, more important, persuasive and memorable) advertising or promotion, or special attention to some aspect of service – it must always be there, bringing something new to bear to combat unpredictable competitive pressures and changing customers attitudes and expectations.

And, last and perhaps of special relevance in a book designed, in part, to present marketing to those outside its function, the fifth C is *culture*. Marketing is, above all, dependent on people; not only the people in marketing – the researchers, the marketing manager, sales manager, public relations executive and more – but the many others throughout an organisation who are, in fact, involved in the process. Some are involved in an obvious way, like those in customer care: anyone who handles a customer enquiry (or complaint), provides information, support or after-sales service contributes. Others may be a little more removed, but still have influence – for good or ill; how many internal policies smooth internal operation but reduce the service or quality experienced by customers? Success is surely heavily influenced by the ability of various combinations of people to work constructively and effectively together. What is more, senior management in any organisation should not only recognise this, but work to ensure everyone contributes knowingly and positively; better still, that as they do so they understand why and get satisfaction from the contribution they are able to make.

The starting point for all this is surely an understanding of the organisation and its customers in a marketing context – and understanding how marketing affects every individual.

Beyond that we must recognise that nothing is static. Exciting and dynamic times lie ahead for many, perhaps most, organisations whatever their field of operation. Marketing is at the sharp end, the people in the function must meet new realities with new approaches, recognising that perpetuating the *status quo* is simply not a viable option.

Of one thing we can be sure: whether a particular organisation operates in a way that ensures it obtains its share of the potential revenue and profit that can come from future markets will depend, in major part, on the view it takes of marketing and how it acts to implement it and make it work successfully.

And marketing people need all the help they can get. In an organisation where marketing is understood by all, the chances of everyone working together and of this influencing success are great. If this book helps influence that kind of wide understanding even a little then it will have made a practical contribution. Ultimately a marketing-orientated culture can play a key rôle, helping generate success and producing the profits which pay everyone's salary; and revenue and revenues have only one source – they can only originate in the market, outside the organisation.

# *Acknowledgements*

No one writes a book of this sort without drawing on many influences and experiences. In writing about marketing I am particularly grateful to those with whom I have crossed paths on training assignments over the years – both clients and, more particularly, course participants. Their comments and involvement have certainly influenced the way I now seek to explain marketing matters.

I would also like to acknowledge my time with the Marketing Improvements Group which introduced me to the world of consultancy and training and gave me so much experience (without which setting up my own firm in 1990 would not have been possible). I first wrote about marketing under their auspices and no doubt my style of explanation still draws on material originally compiled while working with them.

I have also drawn a little on my earlier marketing books, particularly *Marketing Professional Services* and *Marketing on a Tight Budget* (this latter directed at small businesses).

All my writing has been informed by working with talented colleagues and associates; indeed this continues to assist all I do. My thanks to them all.

Patrick Forsyth